After
the Beyond

After the Beyond

*Human Transformation
and the Near-Death
Experience*

CHARLES P. FLYNN

PRENTICE-HALL, Inc.
Englewood Cliffs, New Jersey 07632

Printed in the United States of America.

Library of Congress Cataloging-in-Publication Data

Flynn, Charles P.
After the beyond.

Bibliography: p.
Includes index.
1. Near-death experiences—Religious aspects.
2. Spiritual life.   I. Title.
BL535.F59   1985   236'.2   85-16720
ISBN 0-13-018342-3

1 2 3 4 5 6 7 8 9 10

To Jesus, the Universal Christ

And to those who directly and indirectly shared their
now-eternal Love and Knowledge with me
and who, with Him, made this book possible:

My father, Charles James Flynn

Iola and Clarence Calsen
Michael Hearne McKittrick
Stephen Mansfield Jenks
Thomas Wolfe
Ernest Becker
Linda Colleen Leebrick
Lloyd "Sonny" Goodwin
Clara Haag

Acknowledgments

Grateful acknowledgment is made to Macmillan & Co., Publishers (New York), for permission to reprint excerpts from *Escape from Evil* by Ernest Becker, copyright 1975 by Marie Becker; to Harper and Row, Publishers (New York) for permission to publish an excerpt from *You Can't Go Home Again* by Thomas Wolfe, copyright 1934, 1937, 1938, 1939, 1940 by Maxwell Perkins as Executor, copyright renewed 1968 by Paul Gitlin; to Confucian Press for permission to reprint excerpts from *At the Hour of Death* by Dr. Karlis Osis and Dr. Erlendur Haraldsson, copyright 1977 by Dr. Karlis Osis and Dr. Erlendur Haraldsson; to the Public Broadcasting Council of Central New York for permission to use the quotation by Philip Caputo from the documentary "Now Tell Us All about the War," produced by Nancy Roberts; to the Plough Publishing Co. for permission to use the quotation from *Eberhard Arnold: A Testimony From Church-Community of His Life ad Writings;* and to the many people who graciously allowed me to share their NDE-related and Love Project letters and journals. Scripture quotations marked "NIV" are from the Holy Bible, New International Version, copyright 1973, 1978 by the International Bible Society (New York), and are used by permission.

Contents

Foreword
by Raymond A. Moody, Jr., M.D., xi

Preface, *xiii*

Chapter 1

Beyond the
Final Barrier
1

Chapter 2

The Love
of the Light
9

Chapter 3

Sharing the Experience
15

Chapter 4

Living in Two Worlds
23

Chapter 5

New Priorities and Changed Lives
33

Chapter 6

Close Calls: Do Non-NDEr Survivors Change?
53

Chapter 7

God of Love, God of All
65

Chapter 8

Universal Christ
79

Chapter 9

Lives of Love
101

Chapter 10

The Love Project
119

Chapter 11

Living in
the Light
151

Afterword

by Kenneth Ring, Ph.D., 161

Tables

Table 1. Attitude and Value Changes among NDErs, *166*
Table 2. Attitude and Value Changes among Non-NDEr Survivors, *167*
Table 3. Attitude, Value, and Personal Growth Changes among Love Project Participants at End of Course, *168*
Table 4. Attitude and Value Changes among Love Project Students One Year Later, *169*

Appendices

Appendix 1. Love Project Guidelines, 172
Appendix 2. Student Instructions for the Love Project, 175

Bibliography, 181

Index, 185

Foreword

What you are about to read is a beautiful and, in my opinion, an important book. Although my wonderful friend Chuck Flynn has done me the honor of asking me to write a foreword to his remarkable essay, I don't want to be so long-winded as to tire or to distract you, his readers, before you begin *After the Beyond*.

Let me limit myself to a few brief remarks. In the ten years that have gone by since *Life after Life* was written, many physicians, psychologists, sociologists, nurses, and other professionals have taken the time to listen patiently and sympathetically to large numbers of persons who, having come very close to death, have nonetheless survived and have described so-called Near-Death Experiences. Through the efforts of the many scholars who have now published their findings, the pattern and content of these experiences—the floating beyond one's body and the witnessing of the resuscitation measures from above, the passage through a portal into a realm of light, the panoramic review of one's life, the reunion with one's deceased relatives—are now so widely disseminated and discussed in our society as almost to have become an item of general knowledge.

What is now coming into focus is the spiritual impact these experiences have upon the lives of the people who have them. What these people tell us, quite simply, is that in those moments in which they were apparently dying, they were learning—or realizing—that joy and happiness and fulfillment in life have to do with love. Chuck Flynn has taken his message to heart and has promulgated it in a unique way. What has resulted is something profound. Those of his readers who will listen, and have courage, stand to learn a powerful truth. They will come to realize that the opposite of love is nothing else but fear and that when we let go of our fear of our fellow human beings there opens up an immense vista of the greatest beauty it is possible to behold.

RAYMOND A. MOODY, JR., Ph.D., M.D.

Dr. Moody is the author of *Life after Life* and *Reflections on Life after Life*.

Preface

Death is a cloud hovering over us all. At times, it is a dark storm cloud, full of ominous threat. At other times, it drifts lazily across the sky, and we remain largely unaware of it.

But our happiest moments are when the clouds unexpectedly allow the sun to shine through, bathing us in unexpected light and warmth. At such times we are reminded what has been above and beyond the clouds all along.

Throughout history, people have tried to understand the great mystery of death. Science and technology have extended our lives and made them more comfortable in many ways. Yet they have also provided the basis for the possibility of the total extinction of life on this planet.

Biomedical science has developed new capacities to bring people back from conditions that would have proven fatal in earlier times. Nearly a third of people so revived have told extraordinary stories of lifting above and separating from their bodies, going through a long tunnel at a rapid rate of speed, and encountering a Being of Light, which they describe uniformly as total love and total peace beyond any familiar human experience and inexpressible in human terms.

We are wont to dismiss claims of such experiences. Our scientific skepticism tells us they must be explainable as dreams, hallucinations, or perhaps the effects of lack of oxygen. But when we begin listening to those who have had such experiences and when we see how their lives have been totally, completely, and pemanently transformed, we are intrigued.

What do they tell us? That learning to love others is what life is all about. That the values and aspirations we had thought meaningful pale in comparison with the eternal importance of love.

These are things that sound quite familiar. When we look at what has really meant the most to us in our lives, we find that it has been our deep yearning for the love of others, our great happiness in receiving it, and our deep fulfillment in giving it.

This book looks closely at what many Near-Death Experiencers (NDErs) have to say about life, death, and most importantly, love. It also looks at an attempt to create the same kind of transformations in people who have not come close to death or had any sort of extraordinary experiences but who have tried to apply the lessons of love learned from NDErs by relating in a loving way, to another person whom they wouldn't otherwise have related to. *After the Beyond* shows that the Near-Death Experience can serve as a sunbeam through the clouds that can illuminate and warm our lives and lead us toward the Light.

In a very real sense, this book belongs to the many Near-Death Experiencers, researchers, and students both named and unnamed who are quoted or who otherwise added their insight, knowledge, and love to it. I owe most to Kenneth Ring, whose immediate extension of friendship to someone who wrote to him as a result of an appearance on a talk show so clearly reflects the love of the Light. I am also deeply grateful for the indispensable help of: Bruce Greyson, Raymond and Louise Moody, Nancy Evans Bush, and the many new and deep friendships I have made through the International Association for Near-Death Studies with Boyce and Sharon Batey, John Alexander, Kim Clark, John Migliaccio, Ken Hurst, Robert Sullivan, Barbara Harris, Jim Crum, Leslee Morabito, Maria Castedo, John Audette, and Nina Helene. All helped immeasurably in bringing the many different strands of the love that is conveyed here together, not the least by their own love.

After the Beyond could not have been undertaken without the profound insight and love of Marilyn Adams, who helped me conceptualize it and get through the first difficult stages of implementing it. Her deep love is reflected in much of the benefit the project has brought to others. I also owe immense thanks to the many students who responded positively and lovingly to a new educational idea. So many are not named here, but the book is really in the deepest sense the expression of the profound growth many underwent, which provided me with much growth and fulfillment as well.

I owe a great debt of gratitude to my mother, Cornelia Flynn, for giving me not only much love but a good deal of insight and encouragement, and to my wife, Betty, and my sons, Matthew, Joey, and Jamey, who have allowed me to give and receive love.

Most of all, I want to thank my friend and agent, John White, whose encouragement and love reflect the Light he helps others move toward.

This is the message we have heard from him and declare to you: God is light; in him there is no darkness at all.

1 John 1:5 (NIV)

This is the message you heard from the beginning: We should love one another.

1 John 3:11 (NIV)

God is love. Whoever lives in love lives in God, and God in him.

1 John 4:16 (NIV)

And now I will show you the most excellent way.

If I speak in the tongues of men and of angels, but have not love, I am only a resounding gong or a clanging cymbal. If I have the gift of prophecy and can fathom all mysteries and all knowledge, and if I have a faith that can move mountains, but have not love, I am nothing. If I give all I possess to the poor and surrender my body to the flames, but have not love, I gain nothing.

Love is patient, love is kind. It does not envy, it does not boast, it is not proud. It is not rude, it is not self-seeking, it is not easily angered, it keeps no record of wrongs. Love does not delight in evil but rejoices with the truth. It always protects, always trusts, always hopes, always perseveres.

Love never fails. But where there are prophecies, they will cease; where there are tongues, they will be stilled; where there is knowledge, it will pass away. For we know in part and we prophesy in part, but when perfection comes, the imperfect disappears. When I was a child, I talked like a child, I thought like a child, I reasoned like a child. When I became a man, I put childish ways behind me. Now we see but a poor reflection; then we shall see face to face. Now I know in part; then I shall know fully, even as I am fully known.

And now these three remain: faith, hope and love. But the greatest of these is love.

Corinthians 12:31; 13:1–13 (NIV)

Love each other as I have loved you.

John 15:12

. . . . whatever you did for one of the least of these brothers of mine, you did for me.'

Matthew 25:40 (NIV)

1
Beyond
the
Final Barrier

How would people live if they were free from the fear of death? What would they tell us about life?

Since 1975, with the publication of Raymond Moody's *Life after Life,* a phenomenon that has come to be known as the Near-Death Experience (NDE) has captured increasing public attention. Continuing advances in biomedical technology have enabled many persons who previously would have died to be clinically dead for short periods of time and resuscitated. About two-thirds of these people remember nothing. The other third, however, report lifting out of their bodies, watching what was going on from above, entering a dark void, moving through a tunnel at a rapid rate of speed, and encountering a Being of Light of overwhelming love who reviews their previous lives and inculcates in them a strong desire to help others.

In 1982 George Gallup, Jr., estimated that more than 8 million American adults, 23 million adults worldwide, have had such experiences. Yet few talk about them. Our scientific age is skeptical of anything having to do with the supernatural. Ironically, however, NDEs are a byproduct of scientific advances that enable increasing numbers of people to be brought back from clinical death.

Moody's book opened up a new field of inquiry. Intrigued by Moody's findings, the psychologist Kenneth Ring, through hospital referrals, found many others who had had similar experiences and undertook an in-depth study of NDEs, which led to his first book on the topic, *Life at Death* (1980). A cardiologist, Michael Sabom, at first skeptical, came across many NDErs among his heart patients and also studied them extensively in *Recollections of Death* (1982). Soon after, extensive data on NDErs appeared in George Gallup, Jr.'s *Adventures in Immortality* (1982).

In conjunction with colleagues, Ring established the International Association for Near-Death Studies (IANDS), headquartered at the University of Connecticut. IANDS undertakes and coordinates NDE-related research; publishes a newsletter, *Vital Signs,* and an academic journal, *Anabiosis;* helps NDErs deal with their experience through correspondence and local chapters; sponsors workshops for professionals dealing with NDEers; and serves as a source of NDE-related information for the public.

My involvement with near-death studies began before I knew of IANDS. In 1975, I read *Life after Life* and its sequel, *Reflections on Life after Life,* and was moved by the depth of the love NDErs had experienced, particularly in their encounters with the Light. I was especially intrigued with the view of morality and ethics implicit in these encounters. As Moody pointed out, not only witnessing but *experiencing the effects and consequences* of what one has done to others—positive and negative—seemed a perfect kind of justice. The understanding and forgiveness of the Light also squared with what I knew of Christ's purpose on the Cross of providing forgiveness for *all.*

My work as a sociologist has acutely sensitized me to the great chasm between the way people actually think and behave and what they profess to believe in. Whereas there are countless church members and adherents of other faiths who carry out Christ's teachings of love and compassion whether or not they are nominally Christian, organized religion often seems to separate people through competing systems of belief and by legitimating and rationalizing existing patterns of inequality and injustice directly contrary to the Golden Rule and the love of God and neighbor that are at the heart of Christian and other religious teachings.

As a student at the University of California at Berkeley from 1962 to 1968, I witnessed firsthand the efforts of many of my generation to create a more loving world. I participated in some of these endeavors, including numerous civil rights marches, but soon became disillusioned with the self-righteousness, judgmentalism, and self-indulgence pervading many of the social, cultural, and political movements of the time.

In 1965, I had the good fortune to take a class from Ernest Becker, who was then a lecturer in the sociology department. Becker's profound insights plumbed the depths of society and the human condition. But it wasn't until several years later, when I was launched on my own teaching career, that the full extent of Becker's contribution became apparent to me.

In his last two books, the Pulitzer Prize–winning *Denial of Death* (1973) and its sequel *Escape from Evil* (1975), both of which appeared soon after he died an untimely death of cancer in March 1974 at the age of forty-nine, Becker viewed human motivation as anchored in a universal desire to transcend the limits of organic existence. Becker maintained that human beings are motivated, at bottom, by a desire to achieve meaning and purpose in life by leaving something behind. He called this *immortality striving,* and the means whereby we hope to transcend our ultimate fate—such as money, competitive victory, success, fame, heroic triumph, and countless others—he called *immortality vehicles.* In Becker's view, "what people want in any epoch is a way of transcending their physical fate, they want to guarantee some kind of indefinite duration, and culture provides them with the necessary immortality symbols or ideologies; societies can be seen as structures of immortality power" (1975:63).

Children are important immortality vehicles, particularly in cultures that venerate parents and ancestors. Technological and other artifacts of all kinds, such as machines and scientific and musical instruments, extend the range and power of our bodies.

Immortality striving has had many positive consequences. Throughout history individuals have made scientific discoveries and inventions, written great music and poetry, constructed monumental buildings, and left countless other legacies that have benefited others. The young Chopin, for example, knowing he had an incurable illness, spent the rest of his short life composing music he knew would remain forever.

Many kinds of immortality vehicles, however, can have mixed or negative consequences. The pursuit of unlimited wealth has resulted in philanthropic contributions but has also frequently left victims in its wake. Likewise, although much positive human energy and inspiration are unleashed and engendered through competitive striving, viewing the purpose of life in terms of "getting ahead" implies others are left behind.

People attach themselves to leaders, causes, religions, and ideologies promising future glory. Even if one dies, one has contributed to the great fulfillment and has thereby gained immortality. But what of those who don't accept the truth? Bringing about their demise, however brutally, is honored as heroic victory over the forces of evil. Hence the eternal paradox of hate and destruction in the service of good.

Where does this leave us? In the prefatory note of his last book, Becker's wife Marie writes that he didn't want the book published because he felt he hadn't resolved the dilemma he had uncovered. Is there, in fact, no "escape from evil"?

BEYOND IMMORTALITY STRIVING

Despite the substantial, growing amount of scientific evidence supporting its validity, the Near-Death Experience is still regarded by most of the scientific community and a good deal of the public as a curiosity. Skeptics dismiss it as a form of elaborate hallucination ultimately explainable in biochemical or psychological terms. Those who are less skeptical either focus on the experience itself, with its sensationalistic aspects, or like many fundamentalists, see it as a demonic deception involving Satan disguising himself as an angel of light (2 Corinthians 11:14).

A breakthrough occurred with the publication of Kenneth Ring's second book, *Heading toward Omega* (1984). For the first time, attention was directed not at the experience itself but at the *effects* it has on those who undergo it. In impressive detail, Ring described how NDErs undergo substantial value transformations toward greater caring, compassion, and acceptance of others.

Moreover, in line with Becker's insights, these changes seemed to stem from NDErs' decreased fears of death. A full 86 percent of a sample of NDErs (see Appendix 1) Ring and I studied said their NDEs led to strongly decreased fear of death; the remainder indicated some decrease.

The implications of this are enormous. Psychologists and sociologists have traced many of our individual, as well as societal, problems to anxieties related to death. A psychologist NDEr who prior to his experience had adopted a very secularistic approach in his practice stated afterward that he believed his clinical efforts, and his life as a whole, would be fulfilled if he could fully transmit his newfound freedom from fear of death to just one patient or other person.

An NDEr who has helped many people dying of terminal illness said, "I lost my fear of death, which is a marvelous gift. Life has been so different since the experience. It's as if, 'What do I have to be afraid of?' It opened me up to everything. Why do I have to live within this little shell? I could be anything I want to be, because I have nothing to fear. Death holds no fear for me anymore. And certainly that has to be the ultimate fear—the fear of death."

As this book will show, such freedom from fear leads to indifference to negative kinds of immortality striving. Like many nonexperiencers who have also "seen the light," NDErs engage in a wide variety of compassionate activities. They thus provide a seedbed for the possible trancendence of immortality striving of the more destructive kind in favor of human endeavors that fulfill one not at others' expense but through helping fulfill them.

I met Ring in 1981 and found that he shared my interest in the connections between Becker's ideas and the significance of NDErs' transformations. The following summer, working through IANDS, I began interviewing many of the same NDErs Ken had come to know, plus many he hadn't talked with. In addition, since then, I have come across and interviewed about two dozen more NDErs. In all, including those NDErs I discovered through IANDS, this book is based on interviews with approximately four dozen NDErs. I also had the help of many researchers and scholars in the field, who provided me with various kinds of insights based on their extensive studies of dozens of other NDErs.

Some of the NDErs you will meet in this book have previously talked about their experiences extensively. Tom Sawyer, whose core experience took place when the pickup truck he was working under fell on his chest, has appeared on numerous television programs. Barbara Harris is currently very active as an officer of IANDS and has also discussed her experience publicly on numerous occasions. Elaine Winner wrote to me in response to an article about my research in a nearby city newspaper. She has recently become active in forming IANDS local chapters and has given a number of public talks about her experience.

Others quoted in this book, however, have never discussed their experiences before, and I have given many of them pseudonyms or quoted them anonymously because they are concerned that their families and friends might react negatively to public discussion of their experiences.

As my study progressed, and particularly after Ken published his findings, I began to see that all of the previous books and research on NDEs were part of a progressive unfolding of ever greater understanding of the meaning of the experience.

As Ken had shown with substantial research findings, the after effects of the NDE are very real. The experience turns people's lives around. But what about those of us who have never come close to death? In *Heading toward Omega,* Ken introduced Nancy Clark, a person who had an NDE-like experience while delivering a eulogy for a friend who had died in a plane crash. Nancy's life changed in ways very similar to NDErs' transformations. Love and caring for others became her only meaning in life.

Since she lives not far away, I have been fortunate enough to know and work closely with Nancy. As my work with her and others progressed, it became increasingly clear that *the meaning of the NDE lies not only in the effect it has on experiencers themselves but in the effects they have on those of us who haven't had any sort of transcendent experience and, ultimately, in their effect on the world as a whole.*

Building on the firm foundation of Ken's work, in conjunction with his view that NDE represents a new stage in human evolution, I focused my work on the various ways NDErs affect others. I found countless acts and expressions of love, compassion, and benevolence, some of which are recounted here.

But a basic question remained: Does one have to have an experience to live a life of love and compassion? Obviously, many others who have not had transcendental experiences, or at least have not talked about them, engage in similar actions and have similar loving outlooks. As this book will show, *the NDE is not really about death but about life. The new joy of living for others as well as themselves that NDErs exhibit is a beacon reaffirming what is truly important in human existence.* It can, and has, inspired others who have not had any kind of transcendent experience to carry out the message and mandate of the Light by living lives of love.

With this view of the meaning of the NDE, I decided to attempt to see how the lessons of love stemming from the NDE could be translated into an educational experience. Using Leo Buscaglia's book *Love,* which conveys much the same message, I asked my students to relate in a loving manner to someone they wouldn't otherwise relate to, using *Love* as a guide. In addition to tapes of Leo's talks, I showed them videotapes of NDErs talking about how the experience had led them to be more loving and compassionate. The results, as the last part of this book will show, were and continue to be moving and heartening.

This book begins with a look at the Near-Death Experience in the words of a number of NDErs. Chapter 3 examines the kinds of problems NDErs have in getting people even to listen to them, much less accept the validity of their experiences. Chapter 4 focuses on the difficulties NDErs encounter incorporating the experience into their lives. Chapter 5 looks closely at some of the substantial value transformations NDErs undergo and provides two in-depth, extensive case studies of remarkable changes in the lives of two men who were very different before their experiences.

Chapter 6 looks at research aimed at finding out whether coming close to death without having an NDE leads to transformation. Chapter 7 begins to examine various religious aspects of the NDE, with emphasis on how NDErs adopt a universalistic attitude centered on a strong commitment to a God of unconditional love. Chapter 8 focuses on the implications of the NDE for Christian belief in the uniqueness of Christ. As this chapter shows, NDErs believe in what might be termed a Universal Christ; they share many views of Christian belief but in a universalistic way that avoids sectarianism and affirms the worth of all religious traditions.

Chapter 9 looks closely at what, in my view, is a central meaning of the NDE: the positive consequences NDErs have on the lives of nonexperiencers, to whom they channel the love of the Light they were imbued with during their experience. Chapter 10 switches gears, attempting to answer the question: What does this all mean for people who haven't had any sort of transcendent or death-related experience and haven't been influenced by anyone who has? Citing many students' experiences, I here present some of the more significant results of an educational experiment—the Love Project—I conducted in several classes in which I tried to give my students an opportunity to become more loving and caring in a way similar to the kind of unconditional love promulgated by NDErs but in a context not directly related to the NDE. The results, as you shall see, were often beautiful and profound.

Finally, I try to place the NDE and the Love Project in a broader intellectual and historical context by examining what it might mean in terms of new views of the universe, existing ideologies, the need to overcome war, and the overall attempt to create a more loving world. As the book as a whole shows, the NDE and efforts like the Love Project that it inspires might provide a seedbed for large-scale transformation in a world close to annihilation through forces opposite to those of the love of the Light.

2

The Love
of the
Light

The Near-Death Experience is a life-changing event with a profound, lasting impact. It usually occurs during a medical emergency in which a person either is declared clinically dead or has lost all vital signs. In recent years, advances in biomedical technology have brought people back from conditions that would have been fatal not long ago.

The experience involves a number of stages that not all experiencers undergo. Those who do go through all the stages are what Kenneth Ring terms "core experiencers." The stages, in their usual order, follow:

1. Lifting out of one's body and being able to look at the resuscitative efforts going on.
2. Being in a dark void.
3. Floating through a tunnel at a very rapid rate.
4. Seeing and communicating with deceased relatives or others (this stage can occur at various points).
5. Moving toward a bright light, which gets larger until the person becomes engulfed in it.
6. Encountering a Being of Light of overwhelming, total love and absolute knowledge.
7. Being asked by the Light about how one has lived one's life.
8. Undergoing a life review in which events of one's life are presented and in which one empathically experiences the effects of one's action on others.
9. Being engulfed by and feeling total love and knowledge.
10. Going through the Light and seeing populated cities of crystal or other dazzling brilliance that contain people.
11. Being given a choice whether or not to return, with the Light emphasizing that the experiencer has unfinished tasks or is needed by loved ones.
12. Returning, either through a rapid reversal of the experience or finding oneself suddenly back in one's body.

A TYPICAL NDE

Elaine Winner is a housewife in her forties who had an NDE in 1976 as a result of repeated, unexpected brain seizures. Her account contains many of the elements mentioned by typical NDErs. Having been given the last rites by a priest while in a hospital emergency room, she was lifted above her body and entered a dark void. Soon she felt herself moving through a long tunnel, gradually approaching a light at the end of the tunnel, which became larger and larger. Soon she began to focus on the Light, which she and other NDErs all describe as the central element of the experience:

> It's not the kind of light you have here; it's brighter than that. It was a very comforting light, and I felt myself moving toward it. I wasn't conscious of having a physical body, and I was traveling toward it at an incredible rate of speed. I got the feeling that "Through me, you'll have everlasting life."
>
> I realized in those split seconds that there's really no such thing as death. The death that we think of is death of a physical body. The inside part of you never dies; that spirit, that soul, lives on.
>
> As I came toward the Light I felt the most incredible amount of love coming from the Light. I felt understanding, I felt forgiveness, such a multitude of things. The love I felt was such that if you can think of the one person in your life who loved you beyond anything, this love [of the Light] can't even be compared to that. This love was so total, so complete, I couldn't believe it.

THE LIFE REVIEW

An engineer in his thirties who, when a student at eighteen, had an NDE as a result of a severe asthmatic attack describes what about a third of the NDErs undergo:

> When I got to the Light, there was a lot of communication. It was sort of telepathic. The Light showed me different things I had done, things that weren't very nice, like hurting people's feelings, and things that I could and should have done, things that I could have done nicer, could've been nicer to more people, helped more people. That type of thing. It was concerned with how I related to other people: Did I care enough? Did I help enough? To care and to take care of other people seemed to be a primary function. And yet I didn't feel that it was showing me these things to condemn me. It was more or less for the purpose of understanding. And the Light seemed to be forgiving, too. It forgives trespasses, so to speak.

The Light may focus on seemingly trivial events in the person's life. Accomplishments, status, awards, successes, and possessions are unimportant. Actions in which the person expressed unselfish love or concern for others are singled out by the Light, no matter how outwardly "insignificant" they might have seemed. As Reinee Pasarow (1981) described her life review:

> As I become one with the Light, I was in a single instant what my life had been and what had been of meaning in my life. The superficial aspects of my life—what I had accomplished, owned, and known—were consumed in that same instant by the energy of the Light. However, those acts in which I selflessly expressed love or concern for my fellow human beings were glorified and permanently inscribed in my life record with total disregard for however humble or fleeting those moments had been.

KNOWLEDGE

NDErs refer to the Light as total love *and* total knowledge, both of which many say they become part of. In Elaine's words:

> Feeling myself enveloped in that love, feeling myself surrounded with the knowledge that came off of it, I felt like I knew the secrets of everything from the very beginning of time to infinity, and I realized that there was no end. I realized that we are but a very small part of something that's gigantic, but as people we interlock into each other's lives like puzzle pieces, and that we are just an infinitely small part of the universe. But we're also very special.

How much of this knowledge do NDErs bring back with them? Patrick Gallagher states:

> During the experience I knew that I would lose practically everything but a splinter of this essential knowledge, this absolute knowledge. But one of the things I discovered is that a great deal of what is essential to understanding we already possess. All you have to do is find it within yourself. In this sense, we have a phenomenal amount of information in us.

ENCOUNTERS WITH
RELATIVES AND OTHERS

Some NDErs report meeting relatives and other loved ones. "Mickey Staccato" encountered a brother who had died many years previously.

Elaine Winner met her deceased grandfather and a woman she had loved deeply who had died not long before. Others, such as Patrick Gallagher, report seeing and communicating with other deceased people, particularly those with similar interests and concerns:

> I knew that all I had to do was approach an interesting person and quite easily and almost immediately understand his or her essence. The other person had the same type of interest, and the result was a consummate exchange of knowledge. Words cannot provide a hint of such knowledge.

> Without reflection or words, I knew them as completely as they knew me. I also understood that everyone was in a state of perfect compassion with everyone else. We were freed from all those contrivances historians often claim to be the causes of war and other conflicts—land, food, shelters. These conditions produced a phenomenal state, for neither hate nor any other disturbing passion was present, only the total presence of love. Since love was complete, it also included slight variants such as consideration, respect, compassion, and interest . . . all of these merged.

RETURN

At some point, NDErs receive a message emanating from the Light that it is time for them to turn back to life. Some report being given a choice. For one older man, this was agonizing, since he didn't want to leave the extraordinary place he had come to but felt his wife still needed him. For younger NDErs, unfinished work and the need to help one's family became overriding factors. An eminent physician who wrote me about an NDE that occurred after a car accident reported that he heard, telepathically, from the Light, "Don't you think you'd better go and finish your work?" Some experience no such communication but merely "understand" that it is not yet their time.

At this point, some feel the experience in reverse. Others find themselves suddenly merging with their bodies again, feeling intense pain and discomfort along with a shocking sensation.

Upon their return, when they have begun to recover from the condition that led to their experience, all NDErs are understandably overwhelmed and want to tell others about it. Unfortunately, as the next chapter will show, they often find that no one wants to listen to them.

THE REALITY
OF THE EXPERIENCE

NDErs emphasize that the NDE is not like any dream, hallucination, or other similar type of consciousness, such as a drug-related episode. One who had done extensive scientific research and was well acquainted with various kinds of consciousness stated:

> I felt, when I saw the Light, "I've found it!" It was just an extraordinary experience. It was an event of *utter* reality. It was *totally* objective, *totally*. It wasn't the type of thing, as in some research I've done, where the subjective part of the self enters. No. It was *totally* objective. And *utterly* real.

At the same time, the experience is both very simple and difficult to describe. As one NDEr stated:

> There's just no way to explain it verbally. You can't describe the tremendous feeling of love. It's just . . .it's just so simple. It really is. It's nothing that has to be dissected or analyzed or categorized or anything.

3

Sharing
the
Experience

Finding someone who will listen is the most significant, and often the most frustrating, initial problem NDErs encounter after their experiences.

Once they have recovered, even partially, from the traumas that led to their experiences, NDErs have an overwhelming need to talk to others about it in order to make sense of it. Most hospital personnel, with a few exceptions, consider any talk of visionary experiences as evidence of hallucinations.

Elaine, for example, wanted desperately to talk to her doctor about her experience but was unable to find even a nurse to communicate it to. She overheard her physician tell her husband, "Don't worry, she'll be all right. She's just hallucinating." But, as all NDErs emphatically state, the NDE is *not* something one "gets over."

Physicians and nurses are trained to look at things in a highly scientific way. A survey by George Gallup, Jr., undertaken for his book *Adventures in Immortality* indicated that the overwhelming majority of physicians do not believe in NDEs. Two typical scenarios:

> I tried to tell my story to my doctors and was promptly sent to a psychiatrist.

> I told the doctor about my experience, and he looked disturbed and startled. He said, "You must forget about that."

> I tried talking to a nurse one time. She said, "Don't talk like that; they're going to put you in the psychiatric ward." So I immediately shut everything off in me, and I wouldn't respond to anyone. It was agony. No one could ever imagine.

Family and friends often are unhelpful:

> Several friends asked me what my experience was like. When I told them, they looked at me like I'd lost my mind.

> My husband thinks I'm nuts when I tell my story.

> My family was of little or no help. They did not, of course, believe me and requested that I not reveal in any way what had happened.

Clergy frequently go along with the medical personnel:

> After my operation, they assigned a nun to me. When I first opened my eyes after being put in my room, I tried to tell this nun about

my experience, because I was so overwhelmed with what I had just gone through, what I knew to be very real. And she reached for the buzzer, which brought the nurse, and I got the shot, and out went the lights.

When I was able to communicate, I asked the nurses to send my minister. I tried to tell him I know I died, I know what God is, and I know what happens to people when they die.

He told me not to talk about it and said that I had been very ill. This went on for weeks. No one would listen to me.

Some NDErs, however, eventually find someone who will listen. Elaine tells what happened to her:

My physician told my husband that I was just hallucinating and would "get over it." What I had gone through was not something that you "get over."

I lived with this and I didn't talk to anyone about it for two weeks. I thought to myself, as I lay there, "Where can I turn, and who can I talk to?"

One particular morning, two weeks after the NDE, there was a voice, and I recognized that voice. When I turned over, I saw that this was the same priest. Somewhere in my vision, in my experience, I saw the corner of his face, and I knew that this was the same priest who had given me the Last Rites.

He could not believe that I was actually alive. He really thought that I had died that night. He asked me if he could talk to me, and I told him I really wanted to talk to him. I felt that I needed someone, a religious figure, to explain to me what I had just gone through, because I felt a very religious aspect off of this, I felt there was something very Godly about it.

For the first time, I opened up with everything that had happened to me—the feelings that I had. And I explained to him things that I had seen, and things that I had seen there in the hospital that it was physically impossible for me to have seen, in other rooms, in other areas of the hospital. It was an ability to be everywhere at once, to operate on two different levels of understanding. And that's where I was.

The priest let me know that I was not alone. He asked me if I had ever heard of Elisabeth Kübler-Ross, and I told him no. It turned out that she was a friend of his. He asked me if I'd ever heard of Ray

Moody, and I hadn't. And he let me know that Ray Moody had just written a book, *Life after Life,* and Dr. Kübler-Ross had written a foreword to this book. Later, he brought me a copy of the book.

IN THE SPIRITUAL CLOSET

Moody's and other researchers' books have proven of great help to many NDErs. There are many experiencers, however, who are still unaware of these books and believe they are the only ones to have had such an experience.

This is highly unfortunate, not only for the NDEr but for society as a whole, since what the experiencer has to share is overwhelmingly positive:

> There was so much love inside of me. I just wanted to touch everyone with love and beauty. I wanted to put my arms around everyone and say, "I love you." But I couldn't. They would have thought I was crazy.

Many NDErs give up trying to communicate what they feel:

> I stopped talking about the experience a long time ago because either I got an envious reaction from people who wanted to have a similar experience or I got an awe-struck reaction from those who were afraid of it. Both reactions were very uncomfortable for me.

Why would anyone be afraid of hearing about such an experience?

> Some people tend to get a little frightened when you talk about God and so forth. It's something they have trouble dealing with. They're unable to understand, so they throw up a few defense mechanisms.

Of people who label him negatively because of his experience, one NDEr says:

> That's where they're coming from. It's not from you personally they feel this way. I'm not so much concerned that they'll think, "This guy is off the wall," or something. I'm more concerned they'll think negatively about the experience, about what I said. To me, that means I didn't tell it right.

NDErs are strongly concerned about being misinterpreted. They have a strong sense of obligation to the Light, a duty to convey the magnificence, beauty, and profound meaning of the NDE, which can easily be dismissed, sensationalized, or trivialized. As Nancy Clark put it:

> The NDE is unlike a memory of something that happened to someone in the past only to be recalled at some later date for some reason. The experience itself becomes a *part* of the individual and *becomes* his or her life. So any rejection on the part of others of the experience itself is viewed by the experiencer as a personal rejection of self. When you say my experience doesn't exist, you are saying I don't exist.

THE RESEARCHER'S ROLE

Researchers such as Raymond Moody, Kenneth Ring, Michael Sabom, George Gallup, Jr., and others have helped legitimate the NDE and have provided an acceptable way for many NDErs to discuss their experiences, often for the first time. One NDEr who had never discussed her experience previously opened up to Kenneth Ring:

> After the NDE, I really packed it away. I never tried to speak out about my experience, even with a priest, before I saw a newspaper article about Professor Ring's research. My husband was the only one who knew about the NDE. Up until that time, I had never heard of others having the experiences. I felt like I would like to tell some people about it, because it was a good experience. I felt bad that I couldn't tell. I think my fear of telling someone and being rejected overrode any other feeling.

This uneasiness extended, at first, to Ring himself; the NDEr stressed in her first letter to him that she was not "crazy" or a "kook" but, in her words, "a very normal person: a housewife with two kids, etc."

It is almost certain that only a small fraction of NDErs have talked about their experiences. This is highly unfortunate, since NDErs represent a substantial resource of love, compassion, and caring along with substantial wisdom, which the world desperately needs to deal with its spiritual, ethical, and social crises. How can this potential be realized?

HELPING THE NDEr

In recent years, the NDE has begun to be recognized as a legitimate experience. A number of medical professionals associated with the International Association for Near-Death Studies have developed guidelines for helping NDErs integrate the experience into their lives.

Bruce Greyson, a psychiatrist currently on the faculty of the University of Connecticut School of Medicine, and Kimberly Clark, of the faculty of the University of Washington School of Social Work, have pioneered in the development of techniques for helping NDErs. Out of their work and that of others have come a number of general guidelines:

1. An NDEr needs someone to *listen*. Though it may sound simple, many NDErs find that others either dismiss their stories, interpret them in terms of existing theories, or refuse to listen in a genuinely respectful way.

2. Listeners should realize that NDErs are initially somewhat uneasy about sharing accounts of their experiences. The experiencer should therefore be assured of confidentiality.

3. Because experiencers are often anxious about what others may be thinking about them, listeners should be assured that having had an experience is fairly common and is not evidence of mental instability. This should not, however, be done in such a way as to trivialize the experience, such as by saying, "Oh, that's nothing; that happens all the time."

4. Listeners should *not* treat the experience as something that will "just go away." Such an approach is futile. As one NDEr put it, "I tried to put it out of my mind, but I couldn't. I was walking down the street one day, and it just hit me about the experience. It was like it was saying, Hey! This is real! Here I am! You *must* deal with me!'"

5. Once trust and rapport have been established, listeners should avoid imposing their own interpretations of the experience. Trying to analyze the experience inhibits NDErs. It is important to remember that no matter how bizarre it may sound, the experience is the most significant, profound thing that has ever happened to most NDErs, and NDErs may display considerable emotion.

6. Despite the overwhelming positive nature of the NDEr, many

NDErs express anger and frustration at the rejection they have met and at having been unable to integrate the experience fully into their lives. In this regard, it is helpful for NDErs to have other experiencers to talk with, because only other NDErs can fully comprehend and share the profound depths of the experience.

In sum, NDErs experience many obstacles sharing the experience with others. But whether or not they find understanding family, friend, or other NDErs to share it with, the experience cannot be ignored or "gotten over." The next chapter will look closely at how NDErs reconcile their "old" and "new" lives.

Living in
Two Worlds

The sharp contrast between the total love and peace of the NDE and the realities of everyday life makes it difficult for most NDEs to integrate the experience into their lives. As Tom Sawyer points out, "NDErs come back feeling this love. At times it's frustrating, because in 'normal' life you cannot experience that kind of love. It's *pure* love, as opposed to any combination of feelings of love that we usually experience."

Once NDErs recover from the physical traumas associated with their clinical death situations, they are often overwhelmed by what they have seen and learned and discover their perceptions of themselves, other people, and reality in general have changed dramatically. One experiencer said, "There was a time after the NDE when I was having difficulty coping with it, putting things together. It's a process. And it's constantly going on. I went through some very trying times, personally, jobwise, familywise. It's like I have the experience *here,* and try to synthesize it with *now,* and come up with some meaningful explanation."

CHANGES IN RELATIONSHIPS

NDErs often feel lonely and frustrated at the inability of spouses, family members, and friends to understand or even listen to their experiences. Painful personal difficulties, including divorce, are quite common consequences.

One woman who had an NDE in her late thirties found her pre-NDE existence shallow and superficial. She was married to a professional man and had all the aspects of the American dream—in her words, "a nice home, nice clothes, a $100,000 home in a nice neighborhood." But after her experience, she had an entirely different outlook on life and found that her marriage simply wasn't viable anymore because she no longer shared her husband's values. She said, "I had been so much in love with my husband. Suddenly, after the experience, he became a total stranger. He had absolutely no comprehension of what had happened to my life."

Though no exact data are available on the rate of divorce among NDErs as compared with the general population, such value incongruities seem to lead to what other researchers and I have informally observed to be a relatively high divorce rate among NDErs. Whereas sociological studies show that many divorces occur because of arguments over not having *enough* money, NDErs' marital breakdowns seem to take place because NDEs no longer share materialistic values with their spouses.

Two young women whose NDEs occurred when they were in their late teens told me that they had broken off engagements because of value changes stemming from their NDEs. One found herself no longer attracted to the type of man that had strongly appealed to her before her experience:

> I admired that macho Marine thing before, but after my experience, I resisted it. It seemed like a game mask, a cover-up. I couldn't deal with that machoism. I realized that my fiancé was resistant to change. And I knew then that I didn't want to stop my life. I had begun to grow a great deal in a short time. Marrying him would have put me back in time, in terms of self-development. Luckily, I met and married a man who really isn't into the macho thing. That was a drastic change for me. I wouldn't have married him before, because he didn't fit into society's macho image.

Largely because of her experience, this person became interested in the helping professions and pursued an advanced degree in counseling, the area her husband is also in.

It would be wrong, however, to conclude that divorce or disengagement inevitably follows an NDE. Many NDErs and other researchers I know are very happily married to spouses who, despite initial difficulties, managed to adjust to the "new person" in their midst, often with a great deal of understanding and sacrifice.

Elaine Sawyer, for example, is a model wife and mother who also works many hours to increase her family's income. While she initially expressed some concern over the great amount of time Tom spends helping others, often at his own (and the Sawyer family's) expense, she nonetheless admires the new direction his life has taken and supports him strongly in every way she can. Elaine says that Tom "helps people all the time. It's like he has a job to do. I couldn't believe that he spent nine full hours on the phone last week helping people he doesn't even know. He spends most of his free time helping people. I don't think he does it for ego. I really think he wants to help people. Unselfishly."

KNOWLEDGE AND INSIGHT

Despite the difficulties NDErs encounter in assimilating the experience into their lives, the NDE has many positive effects. The NDE is not the end, however, but the beginning of a lifelong process.

The strong immediate effects of the experience are illustrated in the comments of one NDEr: "I had grown in leaps and bounds in twenty seconds. Maybe eventually, when I was eighty-two, I would have come to the same place. But I think the NDE accelerated it. It brings everything into a very sharp focus. You really see what's important in your life."

But, as one put it, "just because I've seen the Light doesn't mean I'm *there.*" The profound understanding and insight NDErs gain during the experience *must be assimilated into their lives.* For most people, enlightenment comes, if at all, only after many years of dealing with life's tragedies and triumphs or, for mystics and other spiritual seekers, after lengthy study, comtemplation, prayer, and other endeavors. The NDE reverses this process. It is a sudden infusion of overwhelming wisdom, insight, and understanding that most people achieve only in their later years and for which experiencers are often unprepared. As more than one NDEr told me, not with bitterness but with an ambivalence born of a great deal of struggle trying to integrate the experience into their lives, "I didn't ask for this!"

Nonetheless, NDErs have an extremely positive view of the experience. They stress that the ongoing gains greatly outweigh the difficulties. As one older lady put it, "The NDE was the beginning of a growth process. God wanted me to grow as a person. I gained slow, gradual knowledge of people and things."

Even though they claim to have encountered, and even been part of, "total knowledge" during their experiences, NDErs uniformly report a strong increase in a desire for learning. Before his NDE, Tom Sawyer rarely read any books, but afterward he found himself reading many arcane tomes in the physical sciences and other fields, trying to relate what he had learned during his experience to existing scientific knowledge. As Tom put it, "I have the answers but not the knowledge to explain them. I want to know how to interpret them. I'm not, in other words, sure of the questions. Some of the information I don't understand is very in-depth physics. I have some answers, but I don't have the education to decipher them."

More commonly, many NDErs claim to be receiving various kinds of insights and knowledge, which, in their words, they "recall" from the total knowledge of the experience at particular times when it seems relevant to and necessary for their continuing growth process. As several stated:

> There is an innate knowledge that you come back with, but as the years go by it is spoon-fed to you so you can absorb and use it.
>
> The information comes out at particular times, in different contexts.
>
> For me, the implications of the NDE are part of a process. As time goes on, I become aware of more. Things start to synthesize in my head. It's like I always knew it and am recalling it.

An NDEr in her forties, who, after many years of struggle, developed a life style congruent with her new knowledge and capacities and is now very active in civic and political affairs, put it this way: "Though the knowledge I gained was total, my learning to listen to that knowledge, my learning process of paying attention to what it has to say to me, and *relying* on it, to trust *it* more than myself, is still going on."

NDErs stress that the knowledge they have gained is often contrary to what they learned as part of growing up in their particular society. Integrating the experience into their lives thus involves a process of what sociologists term *resocialization:* learning how to incorporate newfound values, beliefs, attitudes, and behavior patterns that have suddenly replaced old familiar ones:

> We all have the same source of knowledge; we all, NDErs and non-NDErs alike, have it given to us. The difficult part is to take out what has been put in, what shouldn't have been put there, things that are blockages to our finding and listening to that inner source. My actions today are not programmed by other people around me or by society. There has been a kind of "burning out" of all the impurities that had been put into me by society.

GROWTH

The NDE also initiates a continuing process of psychological growth. As one older lady stated:

Before the experience, I was at a point where I was just standing still. I hadn't grown, I was afraid, I didn't like myself. I felt very unattractive, very insignificant, all those things. I had always felt that I shouldn't feel this way, but I was always afraid to get out of the little mold I had become trapped in, that I had built around myself.

After her experience, she underwent many years of growth and development and became a leader in various aspects of volunteer human service work, things she feels she never would have done before her experience.

Housewives often have trouble getting their spouses and children to take their transformations seriously. While the NDEr may have become tremendously enlightened, he, and especially she, confronts the same role expectations that had been there before. As a mother with several small children told me:

Vivid as the memory of being in the presence of knowledge, peace, and freedom in the total sense was, it took some time to learn to use the knowledge I had experienced in my life on a daily basis. There were certain barriers I found in trying to utilize that knowledge. I was changed inwardly, but I was back in my body and back with the same family who expected me to be the same. It took me some time to deal with this. When I tried to talk about it, my children would say, "That's great, Mom. When's dinner?"

On the positive side, many NDErs who are parents say that the experience gave them a good deal more patience with and empathy for their children. Another mother stated, "In raising my children, I can perceive so much more about them—their feelings, the experiences I want them to have."

NDErs also tend to see their experiences as providing them with greater patience and peace of mind:

I felt a lot different inside. And the feeling increased. There was a greater feeling of peace with myself. Before, there was always the worry of what's coming tomorrow. Uncertainty, fear, anger. I had a lot of self-destructive, corrosive anger.

There's a lot of things that just don't bother me that used to. Just in general. Like routine things: "Gee, if I don't get this in on time, I'm going to be in trouble." I don't worry about that anymore.

DIMINISHED JUDGMENTALISM
AND SELF-RIGHTEOUSNESS

NDErs also become much less judgmental and self-righteous. The following comments are typical:

> I just can't condemn people anymore because I know where they're coming from. Even if they're "bad people." Because they're still human beings, you know. And they're viable as human beings.

> My new capacity to see others as human beings means I am able to treat people more equally.

> You can accept any kind of person for himself, no categories.

A newfound ability to empathize with and accept those who hurt themselves and others is also reported by many NDErs, as these comments illustrate:

> It's very difficult for me to lose my temper anymore. I can see the pain in other people's eyes—that's why they hurt others.

> It's just wasted energy to hate anyone. I don't carry past grudges. I don't even dislike anyone. That was a definite change. I now look at them as human beings, and lots of times I feel for them. I wasn't able to do that before the experience. I used to be very hurt by others' catty comments. I would be crushed. But now it's such a freedom not to be affected by things like that.

> If another person I encounter is filled with hate, I can honestly look at him as if he is coming from a troubled life. It stays with you.

Tom Sawyer told me of a dramatic change in his attitudes and behavior patterns:

> I was much less judgmental after the NDE. Before, I was so righteous, so judgmental. "Justice" was so important that I would be doing the policemen's work to see that justice was done. Absolutely. I mean, I would chase people, like a cop does, people who had cut me off in traffic or something like that. A *minimum* requirement of another related to this would be a realization on their part that they had done wrong and that I was right, and an apology for having offended me. I was *always* right; I mean, I made sure I

was right according to the criminal justice system. Since I was in the right, I had done justice, I thought. But that would *never* happen now. I couldn't do that. I couldn't have a situation like that. Anything like that is utterly ridiculous to me now. Now, *nobody* can offend me. It's like water off a duck's back. I have to smile because I never realized how much I've changed since the experience.

NDErs ARE HUMAN

Despite the many positive changes NDErs undergo, they still confront the problems and pitfalls of everyday life. Moreover, their experiences have not transformed them into saints or sages.

Nancy Evans Bush, the executive director of the International Association for Near-Death Studies, emphasizes that NDErs should not be put on any sort of spiritual pedestal:

> NDErs aren't all out there trying to enlighten the planet. They're just trying to get from one day to the next just like anybody else.
>
> It's that old Zen saying, "Before enlightenment, chop wood and carry water. After enlightenment, chop wood and carry water."
>
> We do a tremendous disservice to people by leading them to believe that you have an NDE and it's like the "sacred zap," and immediately all your problems are taken care of and you know everything and you can do everything and can counsel everybody.

Although NDErs gain substantial insight and knowledge during the experience, they often undergo many years of preparation before undertaking the tasks they feel called to carry out. Elaine Winner commented:

> The fact that people have an experience that causes them to say, "I don't want to go the way I've been going, I want to go a different way," doesn't mean they're *there*. It just means they've got a different perspective. They've still got to train and prepare themselves.
>
> We do *not* have all the answers. None of us. I may have been infused with the knowledge and felt like I knew the secrets from the very beginning of time to the end of time, but I certainly didn't bring any of it back with me.

As the NDE has become more generally known in recent years, some nonexperiencers have assumed NDErs must be founts of wisdom. As one put it, "I think there is so much opportunity to have our egos fed as the 'know-all' and 'be-all.' " What makes others believe NDErs have special abilities? In addition to their greater compassion and empathic capabilities,most NDErs report various kinds of psychic powers they lacked prior to the experience.

COPING WITH
PSYCHIC POWERS

The increased psychic capacities NDErs report include (1) *precognition:* the capacity to know something is happening or is about to happen; (2) *clairvoyance:* the ability to observe distant places or events; and (3) seeing *auras* around people the colors of which reflect the persons' basic character orientations. In addition, a small minority of NDErs report various kinds of prophetic and historic visions. Kenneth Ring has extensively described and analyzed NDErs' psychic and visionary capabilities in *Heading toward Omega* (1984:165–219). Our focus here will be on the kinds of difficulties some NDErs encounter integrating newfound psychic capabilities into their lives.

Some NDErs' psychic experiences are relatively dramatic, as in the case of one who accurately foresaw, in great detail, a nonfatal car accident involving her relatives. Others have known about harmful conditions or destructive situations and have had difficulty doing anything about them. For example, one NDEr told me he knew a deadly gas was polluting a nearby plant and harming employees and that no one, including the management, knew about it. Realizing no one would take him seriously if he simply informed the management of what he knew, he successfully devised a plan to let them know about it without causing undue harm to those in charge of the facility, whose jobs might have been threatened by the disclosure.

For the most part, however, NDErs' psychic experiences are relatively mundane. As one commented, "Most of these things have a matter-of-fact quality about them. I just know they are going to happen and don't bother to ask questions about them. Lots of times, it's just little things. I'll pick up the phone before it even rings and there will be someone there."

Such capabilities, however, can and do create dilemmas for NDErs. Knowing something is going to happen does not mean one has the power to stop it or even to inform people about it. As one NDEr put it, "What am I going to do, call the police and say, 'Hi, I'm your local self-proclaimed psychic. Such-and-such is going to happen'?"

Tom told me he once knew the location of a retarded girl who had run away and hidden from her mother and authorities. After a great deal of thought and planning, he found the girl where he had expected to and returned her to her mother. He had been concerned, however, that the mother and the police might think he had abducted the girl; if so, he would have found it difficult to convince them how he came to know where she had been hiding.

Tom Sawyer advises more recent NDErs, "Go through this psychic phase, and have the experiences for the knowledge you can gain from them, but don't identify with them. I've used my psychic powers on occasion to help people, and the results have been beautiful. But I'm not that [a psychic] in an overall sense. It's just that I have an imcomprehensibly greater ability to understand other people and their problems."

5

New Priorities
and
Changed Lives

NDEs lead to profound value transformations. As Elaine Winner stated, "All at once, you see life in a whole different prespective. The NDE adds a new dimension to your life, a dimension that wasn't there before."

This new dimension has two main elements: first, a strong desire to love and help others, and second, a newfound *indifference* to, as opposed to judgmental rejection of, materialistic and competitive success and status-related values.

Our survey (see Table 1) showed that above all else, even decreased fear of death and increased belief in an afterlife, NDErs report strongly increased compassion for (76 percent) and desire to help (71 percent) others. Closely related to these were strong increases in acceptance (67 percent) of others; insight (52 percent), understanding (48 percent), and tolerance (57 percent) of others; and ability to listen patiently to others (71 percent). Most others indicated some increases in these areas.

Statistics, however, cannot fully convey the depth of NDErs' new altruistic commitment. Barbara Harris elaborated on how her NDE changed her priorities:

> Relating to others lovingly and compassionately is where the meaning in life is to me now. I finally found what reality really is.
>
> I feel that before my NDE, I was way "out of sync" with reality. I really had a very unhealthy view of reality. But now, since my NDE, since watching my life review, and living every day of my life the way I'm living it now, reality to me is relationships. It's my relationship with everyone else I touch, and their relationships with me, and then everybody's relationships with everybody else.
>
> The life review is where I can pinpoint my values changing. I know, beyond a reasonable doubt, that my whole perception of reality changed, and therefore all my values changed. The NDE answered all my value questions completely. It summarized for me what is important in life. Giving of love is sufficiently important. A lot of things people think are important aren't. Basically, the human heart is what it's all about, and the rest isn't very important. The NDE confirmed this for me.

Tom Sawyer's new emphasis on helping others is evident in new behavior patterns typical of NDErs:

> If somebody requires help, and I am able to give it, I *have* to give it. Before, I might have had a tendency to help, but now it's a *neces-*

sity. I can't be satisfied without helping people. The last trip I took, which was about 400 miles, I stopped ten times and helped stranded motorists. Before the NDE, I might have stopped once. I had always enjoyed helping people, but before the experience, if I had someplace to go, I would have passed them by. Now, I *have* to help them. Even at my own expense. *Guaranteed* at my own expense.

Another NDEr reflected experiencers' typical newfound "people orientation" by saying, "You become aware that an awful lot of things aren't important—*people* become important."

Closely associated with this new emphasis on caring and compassion is a devaluation of materialistic and success-related goals. While no NDErs I came across gave up most of their material possessions to live ascetic existences, they generally became indifferent to things that previously had meant a great deal to them.

In our study, Kenneth Ring and I found that the majority (71 percent) of NDErs reported either a strong decrease or some decrease in concern for material things, with 52 percent indicating a strong decrease or some decrease in desire for wealth. None indicated any increases in these areas. To a third related question about desire for a higher standard of living, 14 percent reported a strong increase or some increase; this could mean the question was interpreted by some as not necessarily involving a higher *material* standard but a higher overall quality of life.

Elaine Winner's comments typify the responses I heard from many other NDErs:

> The thing the Light did for me, that the whole experience did for me, was pick me up and turn my whole perspective of life around. Then I realized that all the aspirations and digging—that you have to belong to the right groups, the right clubs, that you have to have a home in the right part of town so your kids aren't afraid to bring their friends in, that you have to drive the right kind of car—I realized from the NDE that all of that is just a lot of absolute hooey.

NDErs do not necessarily give up all or even most of their material possessions. Those who do retain certain things they were fond of prior to their experiences have adopted a new attitude toward their possessions.

Joe Geraci, for example, has always been a boating enthusiast. After his experience, he continued this hobby, but with a new outlook:

For me now, it's a matter of *sharing* rather than *taking* the pleasure or happiness. Sharing is something that lasts; once you've taken something, it's gone. I like things I can constantly share with my family or with friends, like this house or my boat. I love boating. [Laughs.] That's no secret. I've had a boat for a number of years. It gradually got bigger and bigger. It was always, "I want a bigger boat, I want a better boat." It was not so much status, really, but something in itself. And I thought that by having it, I would be happy.

But I've found since the experience that having a boat means nothing to me unless I can share. Without that, it's totally meaningless. I have a beautiful home and a lot of nice things, but I can survive without them.

Many NDErs do, however, give up a great deal in a material sense after their experiences. This is illustrated in the life of Sharon (not her real name), a young woman who was already launched on a successful career with a Manhattan interior design firm. To the great astonishment and dismay of most of her friends and family, she gave up her career to work as a volunteer with disabled children. Sharon explained her decision this way:

My career just didn't seem meaningful anymore. I really realized this when I went into somebody's house on the North Shore of Long Island, which is full of those Gatsby-type houses, and was asked if it was all right if the pattern on some pillow was crimson, or whatever. I said to myself, "I can't do this. It's ridiculous. What is a lot of money going to buy me? It's going to buy me materialistic things, but it's not going to buy me a sense of accomplishment." Boy, there was just nothing! And so I just quit.

From a lot of people's standpoint, I gave up a lot. But I feel good about it. I feel like I cleaned out a lot of cobwebs. When I quit, I felt like it had been interfering with my real work [her volunteering]. Other people said, "Oh, what do you mean? You're out of your mind!" That kind of thing. I think the world has a lot of strange values. I think a lot of people are, everything is, too materialistic. It's sad. Years ago, I wouldn't have felt that way. Since the experience, I'm a lot more of a "people person."

Another NDEr, a woman in her forties, echoed Sharon's feelings:

Before the experience, I lived for material things. I was conscious only of me, of what I had, what I wanted. Now, I am more spiritually oriented, with a broad new view of things. I have gradually sloughed off the desire to have or hold material or earthly possessions to any great degree. Now, I'm trying to think of ways to get rid of things.

COMPASSION OVER COMPETITION

Closely related to, and often inseparable from, materialistic values is the strong emphasis that our society and many other societies place on competitive success. "Getting ahead," as a television commercial for a Cincinnati brokerage firm says, "is what it's all about."

NDErs see things differently. While they by no means oppose the positive dimensions of competition, with its emphasis on hard work and doing one's best, they are more likely as a result of the experience to be concerned with the negative consequences of an overemphasis on success as the chief end of life.

One NDEer, a successful professional, related misgivings about the competitive pressures he faces that were not present before his experience. In particular, he, like other NDEs, expresses a newfound concern about those who lose out in competitive struggles:

> I'm sure I was much more competitive before and am much less competitive now. Once you've set up a competition, it's either you or the other person: Who is better? I don't know if we can completely get away from that. I don't know what kind of structure we would have without it, but it might be able to be done in a more positive way. I see it where I work, and through friends where they work—the "dog-eat-dog" and "survival of the fittest" thing. I've become less concerned about being promoted. I don't want to climb over someone to have to get somewhere. Since my experience, I strongly feel I am totally incapable of hurting anyone. It bothers me tremendously.

Two NDErs I interviewed, Sharon and Tom Sawyer, had been champion athletes before their NDEs. From childhood, they strove to be number one and had substantial success; Sharon as one of the leading woman athletes in New York City, who had thought strongly of going into coaching, and Tom as a world-class bicycle racer who missed the Olympics only because of an untimely equipment failure during the trials.

Their NDEs let Sharon and Tom to become not so much *anti*competitive as *indifferent* to it. In Sharon's words:

Before the NDE, I was very competitive. Number one down the line! [Laughs] I felt competition was good, healthy. Breeds strong minds, the whole bit. Now I think it's harmful. There's too much emphasis on it. It just allows for a small upper echelon of people to say that they're good, they're okay. If you're not number one, then you're not anything.

You know, athletes are very self-centered. I was, too. You have to be. It's part of playing the game. I don't know if I could ever get back into athletics much, except for exercise. I couldn't psych myself up enough to psych them out. It's *egotistical* to psych somebody else out. You say to yourself, "I'm number one." You have to, if you want to win. We used to scream at one another [opponents]: "You're the worst pitcher I've ever seen!" [Laughs.] So they'd lose their concentration. It's negative. It's . . . *defeating*. To *yourself*. It's like stepping on somebody else. It's morally wrong. You're manipulating people. Without the experience, I'd probably have been a manipulator. I'd probably have been very good at it.[Laughs.] Absolutely. That's the way I was. I hate to say it. I'm glad I'm not now. Thank goodness I'm not.

Such newfound sensitivity to others, based on a heightened Golden Rule moral consciousness, was also cited by other NDErs. One, for example, told me, "I used to be very competitive before my experience, in grades and in sports. But since the NDE, I've been accused by many of being too sensitive."

I asked Sharon to show me the many medals she had won. She replied it would take her about two weeks to find them, because she had put them away and had forgotten even where they were. Before the NDE, they had been, she said, "precious" to her.

Tom Sawyer, who had been an exceptional athlete in a variety of sports, underwent a transformation in his attitudes toward competition similar to Sharon's:

My general attitude toward competition changed. It could be misconstrued by others, who might think, "Well, you've just become very lazy." I've become "lazy," yes, but more than that, my attitude is, I *honestly* just don't care. When anyone says, "I don't care," it sounds like a negative thing, like, "Oh, I don't give a damn." It's not that. It's just that [striving to become a champion] is just not necessary. It's not only not necessary, it would be a waste of time.

Before, it was an obsession. It was so important that it threatened my marriage. My wife said, "Look, either you're a bike racer or you're a husband and father." Quite often I'd train on the bike ten hours a day. I was also the best in a lot of sports: speed skating, swimming, track.[He still holds a state high school record for the mile.] I wanted to be the best. I didn't want to be along with seven or so other guys. I was very competitive. Abnormally so.

REVERENCE FOR LIFE

As might be expected of people newly concerned about the negative effects of competition on "losers," NDErs display increased sensitivity toward violence in all forms. This takes the form of an inability to watch violence on television and in films, an aversion to hunting in men who had previously enjoyed it, and a disdain for guns and weapons among those who had been enamored of and fascinated by them prior to their experiences.

Dr. Albert Schweitzer based his life's work on a principle he termed "reverence for life." All life, he believed, is created by God and is thus sacred. Any harm done to any living creature, however humble, is an offense against God. NDErs' deep sensitivity to the sufferings of others and their empathy for all forms of life reflect a profound reverence for life.

NDErs find themselves unable not only to hurt others but to watch others being harmed. Joe told me, "When I watched violence on the television after the experience, I'll never forget what happened. I couldn't stand it. I had to turn it off. It was a terrible feeling. The needless loss of life bothered me terribly. My appreciation for life is tenfold. I think I used to be a little reckless before."

Several years before his NDE, before he entered another field, Joe had been, as he put it, a "tough cop." Involved in occasional violence dealing with criminals, he would shake them off and say to himself, "Eh, it don't bother me, I'm a tough guy!" Looking back on this from the perspective of his NDE, he laughs, "I could never do that now. Probably wouldn't last a week!"

Other NDErs also told me they were unable to watch television violence after their experiences. One remarked, "I just can't stand it. It drives me crazy!"

Closely related to this is a newfound aversion to hunting among some male NDErs who previously had found much pleasure in it. This is related to an NDE-induced capacity to empathize not only with other people but with animals.

One young Southerner who had nearly died after being electrocuted while working on an electrical transmission pole had been raised, in a fashion typical of his region, to love hunting. After the experience, his attitude changed dramatically, to the puzzlement and concern of family and friends. In his words, "I don't shoot deer, or hurt animals, or cut down trees anymore, because I can *feel* for them. I can feel their energy. It was like the NDE sharpened all my senses."

Tom Sawyer, who had been an ardent hunter since early boyhood, echoed this:

> I did hunt, and don't anymore. Now I can not only see the animal as a "dumb animal," but I can see it at any level it's functioning at— Mother Nature in its purest form, the *real* reality of nature.
>
> Before, if I had a .22 rifle in my hand, and if there was nothing else around and there was a robin sitting on a fence post quite a ways away: "Well, what a fantastic target! Watch this!" Bang! I would be very accurate and I would kill that robin, and my excuse was I needed a target. In other words, I would kill the robin simply to satisfy my desire to shoot accurately. And that was okay, because birds were so plentiful, just like another ant on the street.
>
> But now I actually make an effort not to step on ants. And I never would shoot a bird. If I was in a survival situation, I would in fact catch some kind of small animal and kill and consume it, but please understand—it gets so mystical—I would actually have to ask permission. That sounds crazy, but what I mean is I would have to come to know that, to use other people's phrases, it was "in the karma" of that animal to become my food. Before the NDE, I would have free will to kill that animal just for entertainment.

Tom's attitude toward guns also changed dramatically:

> I used to be fascinated with guns and weapons. Entertained myself with them. Now all that disgusts me. It represents utter grossness. I think we ought to get rid of them all. Before, I was very much against gun control.

A FORMER GANGSTER'S
TRANSFORMATION

The most dramatic account I came across was that of Mickey Staccato (not his real name), who had been an organized crime operative before his NDE, which took place after a heart attack. During his experience, Mickey encountered the Light and communicated with a much-loved brother who had died many years before.

Among other things, Mickey had served as a "bagman" in charge of collection proceeds from illegal gambling operations and had engaged in other activities, some involving violence. His last crime-related job prior to his NDE was as chief steward of a mob-owned and mob-operated resort hotel, where one of his prime functions was providing sexual and other kinds of illicit entertainment for the well-known celebrities who performed at the establishment. In this capacity, he was in charge of a number of high-class prostitutes whom he often treated roughly. Now he makes a modest living as a member of one of the helping professions and does a great deal of voluntary work. In his words:

> Before the experience, my attitude was that people have to help themselves. You know, if they don't help themselves, to hell with them. I had a pretty cynical attitude toward people. I couldn't imagine myself in any sort of helping profession before the NDE. But afterwards, I'd find myself counseling people. I'd find myself listening to people. They said, "You really listened to me. You really understand how I feel inside." Before, I would say, "Listen, pal, I ain't got the time. God helps those that help themselves. So get your butt out there and help yourself. Because it's war out there, on the street. Make sure you always cover yourself out there, because it's a war."

> Before, I thought, "I have to make my way the best I can. Survive." Whenever I started to feel sorry for somebody, I'd say to myself, "Goddamn it, I'm *not* my brother's keeper!" I was hardbitten.

> But after the NDE, my whole outlook changed. I can feel when people are in pain. Before, sometimes I had to *cause* people pain. I couldn't do that anymore. Before, I had to take care of number one. If I gave myself to a job, in gambling or whatever it might be, I would carry it out. That was the rules.

> I look back now and wish I had done something more to help [the prostitutes he bossed], felt more about them. The situation back

then was just the opposite a lot of times. Many of the street ladies would come to me and say, "Oh, my man beat me because I upset him." In Vegas, I knew guys who would beat up women because they were woman haters. And I'd say to the women, "Well, don't upset him! You picked this life, this is what you've chosen. Hey, you dummy, whadda you stayin' there for? Want your head whipped, then stay there! You oughta know the rules."

Now I'd say those rules ain't no good. They're not good for the human condition. I know this now. Nowadays, when I see or hear about a battered woman, I feel for her, try to help her, see? As far as the guy goes, I figure he needs help. When I look back at this, I can't change how I felt then.

The experience made me more sensitive to and aware of others' pain. I still get very teary about others who are in pain. People I know can't understand that. After a while I just adapted to life and got used to being a little different.

Mickey's transformation is evident in his drastically changed values and life style. As I interviewed him in his small shared office before we drove together in his aging Ford station wagon to a McDonald's, he told me:

Sometimes I sit down and look around at myself and say, "What the hell am I doing here? I could be making ten times this money." But I don't want that. My needs are simple. I'm very content. I could live in one room. I used to have a big Cadillac, a luxury apartment. I needed those things. They were necessary for my identity. I felt bereft if I didn't have them. Now, to tell the truth, it doesn't make any difference whether I make ten dollars a day or ten thousand dollars a day. It doesn't matter, it doesn't mean anything. That's not what's important in our trip here on this earth.

I realize there has been even more of an enormous change in myself, from then to now, in that what I'm doing is to help people; it's not for gain, monetary gain. Right now, I'm up to my ears in bills. I got all kinds of bills. But it doesn't really upset me. I'm not driven for the money itself anymore. I can't do the kinds of things I used to anymore to make quick money. I can't do that. It's not that I now think that God, the Big Thumb in the Sky, is gonna get me. It's something, instead, between Him and myself.

Before, all I had was the loyalty—to the guys I worked for and myself. Violence is the only way people can survive in that subculture [organized crime]. It's too bad people have to live like that. This great revelation I've had isn't going to change that. People are the way they are because of the way they've been raised in their environments: social, economic, political. It perpetuates itself.

The overriding value was honor. Honor. In other words, your word was binding. When I said to somebody, "Will you give me your word?" and they said yes, and they broke that, to me that was like a slap in the face. So then they were nothing. They were little less than spittle, see?

But now, I apply it this way. If I say to somebody who has problems that I will try to help them, then that's my word of honor and I will try to help them in every way possible. Now, unlike before, my word of honor isn't an egotistical thing. If I commit myself to somebody, then I'm going to do the best I can to help them. In any way possible.

Mickey's many activities on behalf of others led people in his home town to ask Mickey to become a Big Brother, but, he said, "I hadda refuse, because, you know, I got a record, and the bureaucracy would've gone insane!"

Not long after his NDE, he broke up with the woman he had been living with for some time, who had admired him for his toughness and ability to make large sums of money. One day after he was out of the hospital, and they were eating lunch, she burst out crying and told him, "You're not the same person anymore!" When he asked her what she meant, she replied, "You're not concerned with things of substance anymore," meaning material things. The relationship soon collapsed.

In sum, Mickey's experience totally reversed his value and his life. It did not, however, render him self-righteous or sanctimonious:

Look, I didn't go get myself a robe and sandals and stand at the crossroads and say, "You're going to hell in a handbucket unless you listen to me." No! I didn't sprout wings or nothin' like that. The experience made me realize that the reality of this world is different from true reality. That helping people is more real than this world.

The experience, however, did have profound religious meaning for him:

There was a lot of introspection. There's a lot of things I did that were real wrong. And I realized this. But during the NDE and after, I looked at my life and said, "It really don't matter. There's nothing

I have to hold onto. The past is the past. I'm sorry for some of the things I did, but can't change them. I can't change the past."

I felt there was a forgiveness factor involved. I found myself reading the Bible after the experience, and I felt a deeper understanding of what the prophets and the New Testament said. I felt I came to know the Bible pretty darn well. Before, I couldn't reconcile what I'd done with the Bible, but after the NDE I felt forgiven.

As Mickey's dramatic turnaround shows, the NDE can be seen as an act of divine grace that reverses prior trends in a person's life and allows him or her to live a new life more in accord with biblical teachings, which are also paralleled in many other religions' moral and ethical perspectives that stress love, compassion, and some version of the Golden Rule.

NDErs' accounts of their own transformations are always interesting, yet there is the possibility that the experiencer might exaggerate the extent to which he or she has changed. How do such changes effect NDErs' families, friends, and acquaintances? The following account shows NDEs have profound, lasting effects not only on experiencers themselves but often on those who witness their transformations.

"A.J."

Another striking instance of the transformative power of the NDE came to my attention as a result of a local chapter meeting of the International Association for Near-Death Studies. A man in his late thirties, Ron, came to the meeting and told of an incident twenty years earlier that had stayed in his mind ever since.

As an eighteen-year-old in the Air Force, Ron was stationed in a remote base in the Mojave Desert doing electronics work. He and his fellow airmen, in their off-duty time, engaged in a great deal of carousing and fighting. Ron participated in this, but no one was more of a "rounder" than "A.J.," a Puerto Rican youth from Spanish Harlem who was very quick with his fists, rather hot-tempered, and a leader in the group's rowdy activities. One time, according to Ron, A.J. was in a bar-restaurant and demanded some other customer's taco. This led to a full-scale bar fight, which A.J. had deliberately and needlessly provoked. This was, as Ron told me, his characteristic way of interacting with people: "He was not the kind of individual you'd want to bring to a family outing; a real hell raiser."

One day, while working with some electrical equipment, A.J. was accidentally electrocuted. He lacked vital signs upon arrival at the nearest hospital, twenty-five miles away. However, CPR was initiated, and A.J. began to show signs of life. He recovered and was put in intensive care. Three days later, Ron and A.J.'s other buddies visited him, and they immediately noticed a change:

> When we went in, it was obvious to us that, for all practical purposes, he was a different person. When I went in, I expected that, if he wasn't hurt too bad, we'd be kidding around, you know, trade insults and whatnot. But when we came in, he just . . . had a smile. You can always tell a phony smile from a real smile; I can. I'm very perceptive that way. I mean the smile broke his face; it was that much of a smile.

> We talked a little bit, and I'm thinking, "What's happened to him? 'Cause this ain't him." From knowing him from before, you know there'd have been insults and threats and accusations about whose fault the accident was, who caused him to get electrocuted by the faulty equipment, and so forth. But there was not one bit of bitterness, not one iota. I remember thinking at the time, "Gee, you take a heavy surge of electricity, and it makes you a different person." It was either that, or I figured he was in shock. Afterwards, my buddies and I asked ourselves, "What's wrong with him? The electricity fried his brain—that's what's wrong with him."

But as Ron and his friends soon found, A.J.'s transformation was by no means temporary. His entire personality had permanently changed, in Ron's words, "a 180-degree direction":

> Probably the best way to characterize it is that coming so close to death made him into a chaplain overnight. I mean, that's the impression I got, because in the service the chaplain is always smiling, you can feel the concern or brotherhood or whatever. He had a real concern for other people after the accident. Even at the time we first visited him, he's asking how the job's going and if anybody else was hurt. And, I don't know how to say it, but usually before the accident, to look at him, he looked like a mean guy. He was Latin, and had real dark, penetrating eyes. But after he took

this shock, I mean, even his eyes were different. He was just a different person, as far as personality or how he interacted. I noticed that on the first visit to the hospital, and I was just a young guy, didn't know much about anything. But it has vividly stayed with me over the years—that visit to the hospital. I can close my eyes and see the whole thing. You could *feel*. . . .

What Ron felt, and what he has thought greatly about over the last twenty years, was the depth of the transformation A.J. had undergone. After A.J. got out of the hospital, Ron interacted with him somewhat but didn't see him quite as much as before:

> The significance at the time was just my dwelling on this change; you know, "What happened?" Why he changed. One change I noticed was the way he talked. He used to talk in a kind of real rapid, slang-type street language; every other word is *m.f.er*, you know. That kind of stuff. It was still the same voice, but what he said was different, totally different. He didn't use all the slang. When you'd have a conversation with him, he'd be real softspoken, without the cuss words. And he would look at you when he talked, and he would listen to you. Before, he'd talk, and he wouldn't really listen to you. But after, he would really listen to you and show a real concern for what you were saying. Also, after the accident, to my knowledge, he was never involved in any fistfights; he never in my presence used any kind of foul language; and he never drank to excess again. He drank a little beer and stuff, but he never overdid it.
>
> Before the incident, I never knew him to be religious; he never showed the least bit of interest. After, he didn't "get religion," so to speak, but he did do quite a bit of off-duty work with the chaplain in our home base. He helped with the chaplain's intramural sports program, and they had a deal where they would help out incoming families with finding housing, pay problems, different things. He more or less became the chaplain's informal assistant. Now, I never saw any specific orders assigning him to the chaplain, but he did spend a lot of his time. Everything he did in that regard was either making life easier for people or looking after their health or well-being. If you had a problem and you'd want to talk, they'd help you out.

This pattern of helpfulness and concern was totally different from the way A.J. had been:

Now, this [change] was immediately after that incident. The day before that incident, if you'd looked at him cross-eyed, he'd have punched you in the mouth. That's one of the reasons it's so significant to me—it was a complete, total change in personality. I mean, just a totally different person.

I asked Ron if A.J. had said anything that would indicate his having had an NDE. While neither Ron nor his friends (nor virtually anyone else) knew anything about NDEs at the time, more than ten years before Moody's book first appeared, Ron has since read *Life after Life* and several books on NDEs and has been able to recognize that although A.J. didn't talk about it much at the time out of probable fear of rejection and ridicule (he was already regarded by his buddies as "brain-fried"), Ron did mention things that seem to indicate, in retrospect, that he had had an NDE:

There was a conversation with a couple of us around, and at the time we asked him, you know, "What's wrong with you? What's happened to you? You used to be one of the guys," this kind of stuff. And he said, "Well, it's still me. There's no difference. Things either look right, or are right." That was the phraseology. And we're thinking, "Ahh, what's this business?" And then he did say, "I saw a light." That was the word "*a* light." At the time, if you said, "I saw *the* light," you associate it with religion right away. I came from a Baptist background, and if you see the light, you're saved, or something like that. So then we said, "Oh, God, now he's got religion!" That was kind of how we evaluated it at the time, but I remember, he said, "I saw a light."

A.J. didn't elaborate on this at all at the time. This was probably because he realized his friends would not have understood:

I'm sure if he did experience what is known as an NDE, and he tried to describe it to us, we would have . . .it would have been terrible, you know. We would have laughed at him, maybe even taken him down to the hospital to make sure they admitted him before he hurt somebody.

Despite this initial reaction, the effect of A.J.'s statement has remained with Ron:

The last couple of years, I've been thinking about it all the time going back. It comes back to me and I think, at the time, I thought that he wanted to convey to us that he had gotten religion. But that wasn't it at all. He said *"a* light" not *"the* light." He never tried to preach religion to us.

The NDE is a fascinating subject to me because of the impact that this particular incident had on me, and how long it stayed with me. The biggest single thing is the change in the personality, because even though I was a young guy, seventeen or eighteen, you know, when I saw a bad guy, I knew a bad guy. When I saw a good guy, I knew a good guy. Even then. And to go from bad guy to good guy basically in a couple of days, is uh . . . I just have never been able to rationalize it.

After reading some of things I've read about NDEs, it's something that fascinates me from that standpoint. If that brief glimpse, or whatever, that these experiences indicate makes that much change in people for what now I interpret to be positive things, I would be very interested to learn about it. The significance of that event is what has stayed with me and is still a very high degree of curiosity for me. In fact, I've tried several times to locate A.J., but I can't seem to find where he lives now.

Like other NDErs, A.J. did things to help people simply out of desire to help, with no expectation of reward. Once, when a serviceman and his whole family were wiped out in an airplane crash, A.J. volunteered to crate up the family's possessions and send them to the deceased man's mother in Detroit. He also visited the man's mother there and spent a good deal of time counseling her, tasks that no one else on the base had been willing to undertake. As Ron tells the story,

He packed up all their belongings—they lived off base in a house—and sent them to the mother. The chaplain handed the job off to him, and he took care of it.

I asked if A.J. would ever have done this before his accident.

Oh, no! No, no. [Laughs.] He might've done it, but he would've filled his pockets up with everything he could've gotten, probably. He did it just out of compassion. He wouldn't have had any other motive for that. He really helped the man's mother. Went out of his way to do things. I remember him boxing up a lot of personal effects and sending them to Detroit. He went way out of the way. Before his accident, I would bet any amount of money he wouldn't have done it. He wouldn't have had anything to do with it. He just wasn't that kind of guy.

His buddies found it hard to understand such actions; they felt A.J. must be doing his good deeds to achieve some end, such as making sergeant. Some even derided him for "trying to get to heaven." They simply couldn't believe in his sincerity:

> No one took him seriously; I didn't take him seriously. But in retrospect, I wish I had been a little more knowledgeable, because I would have really taken what he said to be true; I wouldn't have been skeptical of what he said.

One thing that impressed Ron was that A.J. was not like other fellow servicemen who had "got religion":

> We had some other guys around there that "got religion," and they were different kind of people. They'd aggravate you, all the time trying to get you to change your wicked ways. But he wasn't judgmental; not one iota.

This is, of course, characteristic of NDErs in general, who emphasize love and compassion rather than legalistic self-righteousness. Like other NDErs as well, A.J. developed a strong sense of security and assurance:

> Another word I would use to evaluate this person after the incident would be *composure* or *calm*. I'd love to talk to him and see how he is now.

What caused A.J. to change so dramatically? Though he never said so directly to his friends, A.J. showed all the signs of having had an NDE. His newfound compassion and active caring for others were, in particular, congruent with the typical aftereffects of the experience.

Tom Sawyer spoke for many in describing why he and other NDErs become transformed:

> The basic reason is, I've seen the Light. Anybody who can say that knows the story, knows the whole ball of wax—that helping people is what we should do. That's what we should be like. The percentage of our efforts and lives we devote to serving others has been so

lopsided. Two percent in the process of helping our fellow man, when it should be eighty-two percent.

Understand, I'm not claiming to be a saint. But it's beautiful to help people. That's the whole point. The little photons of Light I can spread—even if it's only one person. To observe the results—the beauty, the love.

Some people seem to require all or most of their lives to learn the lesson that love is the central meaning of life. In a very NDE-like transformation, Ebenezer Scrooge in Dickens's immortal *A Christmas Carol* encounters the Spirits of Christmas Past, Present, and Future, witnesses the consequences of his actions in the lives of others, and becomes generous, loving and compassionate. In Tolstoy's *The Death of Ivan Illych,* a proper, respectable magistrate who has been outwardly successful and happy but had avoided the deeper questions of human existence becomes terminally ill. His horror grows and deepens until it turns into three days of screaming when he realizes the futility of his life. He feels himself falling into a bottomless pit but at the last moment sees a light at the bottom and soon is touched by the love and pity of his young son. Finally, an hour before he dies, he realizes that love is the only purpose, the only meaning. At the end, rather than death, he experiences light.

Emily Webb, a central character in Thornton Wilder's play *Our Town,* dies and undergoes a life review in which she witnesses part of her twelfth birthday and sees the magnificence and universal meaning of everyday, "mundane" existence. Jean Valjean, the hero of Victor Hugo's classic *Les Miserables,* is totally transformed by the loving act of a bishop who forgives an act of theft. Pursued by a police detective who seeks to reimprison him and who symbolizes a morality of punishment and retribution, Valjean is caught, then has the opportunity to kill his pursuer but instead forgives him as he had been forgiven, thus upholding and affirming the inevitable ultimate triumph of the morality of grace and forgiveness over legalism and revenge.

For some, the contemplation of death seems to have a significant effect. As the NDE shows, we will experience the consequences of our actions on other people when we die. Can this truth be conveyed to non-NDErs, even those who are very far from the love and compassion of the Light?

A friend whose parents are Auschwitz survivors related to me that his father, a Polish Jew, had once been forced to dig his own grave by a Nazi soldier and was about to be killed. Just before the soldier was to kill him, my friend's father told the soldier, "Someday you will be about to die, and you will remember me." Unlike the pleas for mercy and pity, which the Nazis had hardened themselves against by training and propaganda that emphasized they should be "hard" and "avoid sentimentality," this affected the Nazi. He thought for a moment, and then kicked my friend's father in the pants and said, "All right, you damn Jew, get out of here," and let him go.

This poignant story shows that the contemplation of death, irrespective of whether it is accompanied by an NDE, has a strong effect on people's values and outlook. In her work with the terminally ill as well as others in her workshops, Elizabeth Kübler-Ross emphasizes the importance of "dealing with unfinished business." To what extent does confrontation with death, as by narrowly escaping it or trying to deal with the meaning of one's life when one is aware that he or she is dying, lead to transformations similar to those of Mickey, A.J., and other NDErs?

6

Close Calls:
Do Non-NDEr
Survivors Change?

This chapter will look at studies and accounts of people who have had "close calls" in various kinds of misfortunes and who were, as might be expected, significantly affected. Did their brushes with death change them in ways similar to NDEs?

Overall, the available evidence, though still limited and fragmentary, shows coming close to death causes *some* kinds of change similar to NDE-related transformations. The depth and uniformity of NDErs' transformations contrast substantially, however, with changes in non-NDErs.

RESEARCH ON THE EFFECTS
OF LIFE-THREATENING SITUATIONS

An extensive study of transformations of people who came close to death was undertaken by Professor Russell Noyes and his associates (1982) of the Department of Psychiatry of the University of Iowa School of Medicine, who gathered 215 accounts of people who had survived life-threatening situations, personally interviewing 76 of them. Though Noyes refers to these as "near-death experiences," he does not analyze the content of the experiences to determine how many of his subjects had Moody-Ring type experiences, so it is unclear how many of his subjects had NDEs in the sense in which I use the term in this book. Nonetheless, his findings showed substantial transformations, but they were not as uniform, unidimensional, or universal as among Ring's and my sample of NDErs.

Nearly two-thirds of Noyes's subjects (138 of 215, or 64 percent) stated their close brushes with death changed their outlook in some way. The remainder either reported no change or did not comment. In contrast, virtually all NDErs indicated substantial change stemming from their experiences.

Of the two-thirds that reported change, reduced fear of death was cited by 41 percent. Several referred to feelings of peace and serenity they had unexpectedly encountered during their experience as the major reason for their lessened anxieties about death. This seems quite parallel to patterns reported by NDErs. However, well over 90 percent of NDErs report lessened anxiety over death, and virtually all NDErs report feelings of peace and tranquillity.

Noyes also found 9 of his 138 (7 percent) subjects who said they felt less vulnerable than they had before. Thirty (21 percent) also mentioned a sense of special destiny—that God or some other force had spared them for some special purpose. This, of course, is similar to NDErs' feelings that they were sent back in order to complete some unfinished work. Of the Noyes subgroup, 24 (17 percent) identified God or some other specific agent as the source of this special destiny. One said, "I believe God wanted me to live to provide love and faith to others." This, of course, is similar to many NDErs' statements. Again, however, patterns prevalent among virtually all NDErs are reported by only a minority of Noyes's subjects.

This contrast extends to other kinds of changes in outlook. Only 10 percent of Noyes's subjects reported a stronger belief in life after death. Nearly all NDErs, in comparison, state their experiences provided them not only with enhanced *belief* in an afterlife, but *direct knowledge* of its existence. Likewise, 23 percent of the Noyes subgroup reported a greater sense of the preciousness of life and an attempt to live more fully. In contrast, though no exactly equivalent question was asked of NDErs, all but one in our sample of NDErs indicated strong increase in "belief that life has inner meaning." And, as we have seen previously, the NDE gives people a strong sense of purpose in life, even if it takes time to assimilate the experience into their lives.

Of Noyes's changed subjects, 10 percent mentioned that the sense that life could be taken away at any time led to a greater achievement orientation, a greater urgency to get things done "before it is too late." Some of these placed human relationships and nonmaterial values as newly significant and important, a pattern similar to that found among those whose experiences conform to the Moody-Ring model.

At the same time, some of Noyes's subjects commented that they had less caution and were more inclined to take risks in life in the sense of stretching out to others in human relationships. Others told Noyes that they had less desire to try to control their lives, that they tried to "live from day to day" and "take each day as it comes."

However, 10 percent of Noyes's changed subjects had negative reactions to their life-threatening experience, becoming more fearful of death and more phobic in general, more cautious about life, and more anxious.

In sum, changes generally similar to those reported by NDErs took place among about half of Noyes's subjects. Unfortunately, the data are not directly comparable because Noyes did not ask the same kinds of attitude-related questions concerning greater desires to help others, compassion, and so on as were asked of our subjects.

FEAR OF DEATH AMONG
NDErs and NON-NDErs

Sarah Kreutziger, a social worker who worked closely with Dr. Michael Sabom at the University of Florida Medical Center in gathering the data for *Recollections of Death* (1982), interviewed many hundreds of people who have come close to death and has extensive knowledge of published and unpublished research dealing with how such experiences have changed people. I asked her to comment on her general impressions of how NDErs' changes in outlook compare with those of non-NDErs. In her words, "One definite change that serious illness causes is a change in priorities. Family, friends, health, etc., become far more important, for example, than material things. My guess is that this occurs with or without the NDE, although the NDE may intensify this emphasis. I bring this point up to emphasize that serious illness itself does cause major life changes just by having to go through with it."

However, she also stated the research she and Sabom (1977:124ff.) undertook showed results somewhat discrepant with Noyes's study: "Among people who had not had an NDE, fear of death remained the same or increased after coming close to death, while those who had had NDEs had decreased fear of death." In general, like Noyes, Kreutziger sees some parallels between NDErs and non-NDErs but also some contrasts.

TRANSFORMATIONS AMONG NDEr
AND NON-NDEr SUICIDE ATTEMPTERS

Professor Bruce Greyson of the Psychiatry faculty of the University of Connecticut School of Medicine, in conjuction with Kenneth Ring, has studied a substantial number of suicide attempters, some of whom have reported NDEs and others not. According to Greyson, those suicide attempters who have had NDEs are much less inclined than non-NDErs to repeat their suicide attempts. In both published (1981) and unpublished articles based on a study of sixty-nine suicide attempters, he related this disparity to three main syndromes found in all NDErs he studied but much less frequently in non-NDErs. These factors include (1) the *transpersonal* factor—feeling less isolated from other people after the NDE, feeling "at one" with other people, and a general feeling of cosmic unity with others and with the universe; (2) the *transcendental* factor—a sense that they were privileged to have been saved from death by God and that they had a reason to live,and that God regarded suicide as morally wrong; and (3) the *re-evaluation* factor—a feeling that things that were previously considered important were no longer important.

One element that Greyson, as well as Moody, emphasizes is that suicide attempters who have NDEs come back with the strong realization that suicide is not an answer to their problems. They not only take their problems with them in the afterlife but have little chance to work them out. Moreover, some of Moody's subjects reported that God told them they would have to witness the consequences of their action on others' lives and that they would not "be in Heaven" with God if they committed suicide because it was "absolutely forbidden" to take one's own life and to do so incurs substantial penalties. These, together with the more positive dimensions of the NDE, constitute such a strong set of factors that Greyson and Ring have found a very striking difference between suicide attempters who have NDEs and those who do not. As a clinician specializing in emergency psychiatry, Greyson has dealt with hundreds, perhaps thousands, of suicide-prone individuals and suicide attempters. In all this experience, he has encountered only *two* suicide attempters who had NDEs and who repeated their attempts (neither of which succeeded). This contrasts with a very substantial majority of non-NDE suicide attempters who repeat their attempts and frequently succeed. This is one of the most substantial and dramatic measures of the effects of the NDE. As Greyson summarizes his research, "Though it often takes a good deal of time for the full effects of a suicide-related NDE to be integrated into people's lives, for the most part suicide attempters who have NDEs come back from the NDE thinking that there is more of a sense of purpose here" (personal communication).

NON-NDEr SURVIVORS:
A PRELIMINARY INFORMAL STUDY

Since the study of the effects of NDEs is a very new area, there are as yet no definitive findings on the precise degree to which non-suicide-related NDErs are transformed in contrast to those who come close to death without having NDEs. Greyson and his associates at the International Association for Near-Death Studies are presently undertaking research that will compare NDErs with non-NDErs on a variety of dimensions of attitudinal and other forms of transformation. At present, the available evidence suggests, according to Greyson, that non-NDErs who come close to death undergo some changes similar to those of NDErs, but that these changes are neither as uniform nor as profound as those NDErs undergo.

In order to get a firsthand understanding of how coming close to death changes people, I undertook a preliminary, small-scale study of my own to begin to ascertain the extent to which non-NDEr "survivors" of accidents, serious illnesses, and the like might undergo transformations similar to those of NDErs. Since none of the previous studies had used questionnaire items comparable to those I had used in studying NDErs, I decided to interview non-NDEr survivors and administer the same questionnaire that Ring and I had administered to NDErs in order to obtain comparable data. I found the majority of people through a visiting nurses' agency.

A majority of the non-NDEr survivors, 9/12 or 75 percent, indicated a strong increase (6/12 or 50 percent) or some increase (3/12, or 25 percent) in desire to help others. Similar patterns were generally apparent in other aspects related to helping others (see Table 2). Although these patterns are similar to those of our sample of NDErs (see Table 1), nonetheless there are larger numbers of NDErs who indicate they have strongly increased in the items related to concern for others. Much greater variation between NDErs and non-NDErs occurs, however, in response to questions related to fear of death and belief in an afterlife. *All* our samples of NDErs indicated strong or some decrease in fear of death and increase in belief in an afterlife, the majority strongly. As Sabom and Kreutziger also found, a significant number of non-NDErs experienced an *increased* fear of death as a result of their "close calls," as was the case with one-third (4/12) of my very limited sample. In addition, non-NDErs' belief in an afterlife is apparently not affected much by their brushes with death, with the majority indicating "no change" in this degree. However, such happenings do tend to influence religious perspectives and outlooks, but again, to a lesser degree than with NDErs (see Table 2).

Such results are very limited in their generalizability because they are based on very small numbers and thus can in no way be considered conclusive. Nonetheless, they do follow the same pattern suggested by Noyes's, Sabom and Kreutziger's, and Greyson's findings, all of which point to some similarities between changes among NDErs and non-NDErs. Non-NDErs' changes, however, were not as clear-cut or pervasive as among NDErs. Moreover, among non-NDErs I studied, coming close to death in itself did not seem as important a basis for change as the particular circumstances and situations they faced as a result of their brushes with death, as the following interviews reveal.

The individuals I interviewed ranged in age from seventeen to seventy-five. They narrowly escaped death in a variety of ways, most commonly in auto and other accidents but also through illness and, in one case, war. As might be expected, the older the person was when the life-threatening situation occurred, the less likely he or she was to report any change. For example, the oldest person I interviewed, a gentleman of seventy-five who had a serious operation during which he nearly died, reported essentially no changes. On the other hand,younger people were often affected quite strongly.

One woman was twenty-nine and newly divorced in 1967 when she had a serious auto accident in which, among other injuries, all the bones in her face were broken when her face hit the dashboard. She is not sure whether she was declared clinically dead but knows she was in critical condition for some time after the accident. Her appearance was seriously affected by her injuries:

> I think I had a real bad psychological hangup for years, and I probably still do, because of this face business. The first year afterwards was really bad, because I couldn't have any cosmetic surgery for a whole year because my facial bones had to set and mend.
>
> I can't remember any religious thing. I was thankful I didn't die. I don't remember having a feeling that I had a purpose or meaning in being spared.

Fourteen years later, this same person contracted cancer, and when I interviewed her, she had recently recovered from a cancer operation that had nearly taken her life. She feels her later brush with death, which still threatens due to the unpredictability of her particular type of cancer, has made her more thoughtful and more religious than had the earlier misfortune:

> I've kind of thought a lot about life since my cancer surgery. I've thought about things I'm going to do different. Go to church. I haven't been yet. [Laughs.] I keep saying I'm gonna go. I've done a lot of praying—an awful lot. I thing I'll do better than I've done—not that I've been such a terrible person. At least I hope I haven't been. It has made me think in a religious sense.

After her earlier accident, she felt so sorry for herself that her ruined appearance "was about all I could think about at the time." However, her bout with cancer has, she feels, made her more compassionate toward people with the same problem. She also reported greater appreciation for the ordinary things of life, a less materialistic orientation, and greater contentment:

> You stop and think about the things you've got and things you gripe about, and the things you want, and then you realize you're not so bad off. It could be a whole lot worse.

She also experienced some increase in her fear of death as a result of the cancer, and she finds herself thinking about death quite a bit:

> I've thought a lot about dying. You can't help, you know, thinking about it. It's bound to be on your mind.

She also reports a strong increase in her personal search for meaning in life:

> There must be something else on this earth for me; I may not be able to know it all.

Whereas some people who have nearly died exhibit strong increases in prayer and religious motivations (though not necessarily religious actions) and some increase in compassion and caring for others as a result of an increased capacity to empathize with others who have similar afflictions, others have strongly negative reactions. One of the most poignant cases I encountered was that of a young man of twenty-three who, at seventeen, had been totally paralyzed from the neck down as a result of a motorcycle accident while commuting to a job he held trying to make money for college. Though confined to a respirator, he was gradually able to learn to use a mouth-operated wheelchair, and he has managed to attend college. Until recently, he has been very resentful of his condition and he has been asked to leave several nursing homes because of his abusive behavior toward the staff and other patients. Not long before I talked with him, however, he met a young woman in one of the nursing homes who has been paralyzed for eleven years, since she was thirteen, but not as severely. The patience and compassion she had developed as a result of her condition exerted a great influence on him, and they were married not long after I interviewed them.

A seventeen-year-old girl I interviewed had been hit by a speeding car on a freeway after she and some friends had stopped to help out the occupants of another car that been involved in an accident. She was in a coma for several days and was not expected to live. However, she overcame massive brain damage and now appears and acts relatively normal. Since the accident, she has undergone considerable changes, some of which are similar to those characteristic of NDErs.

For example, like NDErs, she is now much less afraid of death, less materialistic, and less inclined to worry about what others think of her. She says, "I used to look at life like I was a Barbie doll and all I was there for was to look pretty and go out and do things. Now, I stay home, and I don't work at looking pretty or nothing." She also reports having somewhat greater compassion for others: "I don't like to see people down anymore. I hate to see somebody cry."

She has also become somewhat more religious since her accident, and she reports that she prays every day and thanks God for her recovery. However, she paradoxically states there was essentially no change in her religious beliefs, and even though she prays, she still has strong doubts: "It's hard to know if there's a God. I mean, it's kind of silly to believe in somebody I've never seen before. But nonetheless, I feel there's somebody up there watching me all the time."

Like NDErs, she also feels "there's some purpose in my life; there's something waiting for me out there. I didn't feel that way before." However, unlike NDErs, she is extremely impatient and intolerant of other people (which may, of course, be related to her brain damage), and she reports a strong increase in her enjoyment of television and movie violence.

Somewhat similar patterns of change are apparent in a very different case, a man in his sixties who narrowly escaped death several times during combat in World World II. In 1945, Harold G. was in France in a makeshift medical facility with an upset stomach when a shell hit outside the window: "When I came to, I could hear the chaplain saying the last rites. I started yelling, 'Not Me! Not me!' They finally dug me out. There were seven dead men on top of me." This incident increased his religious faith: "It sure proved that the Good Lord was taking care of me, because all the others were dead and I wasn't."

About a week later he was back on the front lines under attack. "Suddenly it felt like my neck had been torn out by the roots. When things quieted down, I took my helmet off and there was a groove right down through the middle of it. The bullet had hit, but not quite low enough. Cut a groove right through the top of my helmet."

In yet another instance, Harold had been forcibly prevented from going into a battle operation by a friend who insisted on taking his place. The friend was killed. The friend knew Harold's son was to be born soon to his wife back home.

As a result of what might be termed his sense of having a "guardian angel," Harold reports he did change in ways generally similar to NDErs. However, he does not attribute these changes necessarily to his close brushes with death: "I'm all the time helping people, but not necessarily because of what happened. I'd been doing that through the church before. I also have an increased ability to listen patiently to other people's problems. As long as I'm listening to other people's problems, I'm not thinking about my own. I'm also pretty tolerant of other people."

He also experienced an increase in religious feelings, a concern for spiritual matters, and an involvement in prayer and organized religion. He had, however, been a strongly religious person previously and, in addition, "had always reached out to others."

Unlike NDErs, Harold became strongly interested in raising his standard of living. He also did not find himself much less afraid of death, nor did he come to believe more strongly in life after death.

Others who nearly escaped violent death exhibit both a greater respect for life and an increased desire to find out "what it's all about." Although I did not interview them directly, two individuals who survived a serious plane crash (they were among only five of more than seventy to survive) commented on how it had affected them in a televised interview a year after the crash. One, a young woman in her twenties, stated:

> I respect life a lot more. I don't take anything for granted. You realize your vulnerability.

> I guess I felt my time hadn't come yet. You're given a chance and you do with it the best you can. I just don't think I was ready to go. They say everyone has their own time, and when it's your time, you go. It just wasn't my time yet.

The other survivor, a man in his forties, reflected a somewhat more philosophical orientation:

> It [the fact of having been one of the very few survivors] keeps com-

ing back to you. I'm doing a lot of soul searching, trying to understand the whys and the wherefores.

I was a Christian prior to the crash, and to me it was a miracle of God that we survived that day. There is no rational explanation why the five of us got out of that plane crash. For me, it's been kind of like living one day at a time, not taking anything for granted. You find out you're not really in charge of anything. And I feel a real need to tell my family and people around me how I feel and demonstrate it every day and not just put it off until I have more time.

I think so many of us get so wrapped up in the day-to-day hustle and trying to be successful that we just don't take time to do it [show love to others]. I think, in my situation now, I try to. I'm not always successful.

These feelings seem quite similar to NDErs' attitudes, but more research is needed to determine adequately how close the parallels are.

Whereas most of the people in my informal study of non-NDEr survivors exhibited some changes similar to those of NDErs, others developed patterns quite opposite to those typical of NDErs. One woman in her early fifties, a successful hospital administrator, was, like some of the others I interviewed, very bitter about a serious accident she had had several years earlier. As a nurse who later became involved in administration, she reports that she always had had empathy and sympathy for those with physical problems and that her own accident increased this somewhat. However, she became very negative toward God and religion as a result of the pain and complications of the accident. In a way reminiscent of Job's railing against God's apparent injustice toward him, she stated:

I was a very devout Catholic before the accident, and I considered myself a Christian. I am now an agnostic. Being a Catholic, I believed in a personal God, and I lost my belief in a personal God. My trying to cope with the accident is what did it. I prayed continuously and intensely for God to give me a sign that He at least heard me, that He at least understood, that if He wouldn't help, He would at least give me a sign that He had heard, that He was considering something, that it was part of a plan. And there was never any sign. So I decided that I was really looking for something supernatural that didn't exist, and that I would have to think more rationally about this. We are so helpless. I was just looking for a straw to grasp onto.

Also unlike that of most NDErs, her desire for wealth and concern for material things increased substantially. However, parallel to NDErs' patterns, she did become more compassionate. Her accident and its painful aftermath of months of rehabilitation made her more tolerant of others, particularly patients:

> Even after my orthepedic surgeon told me my bones were all put back together and the plastic surgeon said he'd done the best he could, I still did not feel well. Before the accident, I had felt that if the doctor discharged a patient, well, then, obviously the patient was well and should get on with life and stop complaining. Now I understand that sometimes your feelings about your abilities to handle things can be destroyed if you walk with a limp or something. It bothers the [handicapped] person more than it bothers other people, but you feel that other people are judging you because of these things.

Overall, there is some evidence that coming close to death without having an NDE changes most people in ways similar to those undergone by NDErs. However, non-NDErs' transformations are apparently neither as uniform nor as profound as those of NDErs. Moreover, there is also evidence that some non-NDEr "survivors" react to their misfortunes in ways divergent from and even directly opposite to NDE-related patterns. Further research is needed, however, if any definite conclusions are to be drawn. Bruce Greyson's work holds substantial promise for the emergence of more definitive conclusions concerning the contrasts between NDErs and non-NDEr survivors.

Although the question of whether coming close to death is sufficient to cause substantial transformations is not yet fully decided, NDErs definitely and uniformly view their experiences as having given them a direct encounter with God. This, perhaps more than any other aspect of the NDE aside from its tendency to make NDErs more caring and compassionate, is a central consequence of the experience. The next two chapters will explore the religious effects and implications of the NDE.

7

God of Love,
God of All

NDErs uniformly say their experiences gave them not merely a *belief* or *faith* in God but a *direct knowledge* of Him. Moreover, they all stress that His greatest attribute is love. In Tom Sawyer's words, "What happens during the NDE is that there is an experience of transcendence of the true, pure love of God. And regardless of who you are and the intensity of your experience, some aspect, some measure, of that love—what the word *really* means—rubs off on you. It becomes part of you."

Patrick Gallagher, like many intellectuals, used to believe, in his words, that "everything is chance." After his experience, this changed dramatically. As he put it, "When I saw the Light, I felt,'I've found it!' It was just an extraordinary experience. I felt that, finally, I was alive. I had this absolute knowledge that was profound, radiant."

Tom Sawyer had a similar transformation: "Before the NDE, I was absolutely an agnostic, a very honest agnostic, in that I didn't pretend to believe in something just to avoid other people's disapproval. I was comfortable as an agnostic. I used to think, 'When you're dead, the show's over. It's just black nothingness.That's all.' Now, I don't know that there *is* a God; I *know* God. All of a sudden, I *know* Him."

Another former agnostic put it this way: "When I had this experience, it gave me some very important things. It gave me the absolute knowledge that God exists, which, before the NDE, I didn't believe in. That was a very special gift. To know that God exists was a marvelous gift for me."

THE INWARD
PRESENCE OF GOD

Closely associated with what they regard as their knowledge of God is a tendency toward inward spiritual transformations among NDErs. While by no means reclusive or introverted in the manner of contemplative monks or nuns or other kinds of mystics of both Western and Eastern religious traditions, NDErs share with them an emphasis on the inner, profoundly deep nature of their religious transformations.

In response to a question asking whether they felt any increase since the NDE in their feelings of the inner presence of God, 71 percent indicated strong increase, 24 percent some increase and 5 percent no change, with no decrease at any level. One respondent added, "I feel even closer to God, and feel Him closer to me. I can also feel His guidance."

Closely related to this is an enhanced sense of meaning and purpose in life, usually centered on being an instrument of God's love. One person said, "I'm less concerned with making something happen in my life. Will God do these things? He already is. I'm here for a reason. And He knows what it is. And I'm very happy."

The NDE definitely causes experiencers to believe their lives have an inner meaning. All but one of our group of NDErs indicated that their experiences had caused a strong increase in their belief that life has an inner meaning, the sole exception indicating no change.

This inner meaning seems closely related to God. The substantial majority of NDErs report substantial increases in prayer, 38 percent strong increases, 43 percent some increase, and 10 percent no change or some decrease (see Table 1).

Overall, NDEs lead to a much deeper, more pervasive belief in God for NDErs compared with their prior perspectives. Many believe God has a special reason for giving them the experience. One called it a "miracle": "It's like having a baby. The experience is wonderful, a God-given gift, a beautiful miracle."

In this sense, the NDE provides many of the same subjective experiences that are associated with deep religious conversions. One consequence is a sense of being much closer to God. Nancy Clark emphasizes that although she was somewhat religious beforehand, her experience gave her a sense of ongoing communion with God, a closeness that is apparent in the spiritual and personal radiance that she and many other experiencers convey. As Nancy describes the effect of the experience on her sense of God's presence:

> I feel such a closeness to God since my experience. In retrospect, I can look back through the years to the time when I considered myself to be "religious." I went to church every Sunday, I spent a lot of time in prayer and so forth, and I honestly thought I couldn't feel any closer to God. I felt I had a deep personal relationship with Him. But if I were to have rated my closeness to Him at that time on a scale from one to ten, I would have rated my closeness to Him then as a ten. But following my experience—and this is very, very interesting—I can honestly say that on a scale from one to ten, I would rate my former *religious* closeness to God as, perhaps, a two.
>
> You see, I'm able to be in a position of having experienced a closeness to God from two different perspectives: one being the religious, and the second, the spiritual, which is the realm I have been elevated to following my experience. If I were to rate my closeness

to God now, after my experience, I'm afraid the number does not exist. In other words, the closeness to God I feel now *is* the actual presence of God in me. I feel His Spirit as this all-enveloping, pure love that cannot be verbalized.

There is a great truth in the Bible's statement that God is love. That has more meaning to me following my experience than before my experience. Because, prior to my experience, I related to that phase from a human framework of love. And now I'm able to see that phrase "God is Love" truly for the truth that it is. His love inside of me is a feeling, an energy, a force—perhaps the name is not important to identify. What *is* important is the *effect* of this love on my own personal life and in the lives of the other people to whom I am able to channel this love. Once a person experiences this absolute, unconditional love, that pure love becomes the focus of his or her life.

THE NDE AND
INSTITUTIONALIZED RELIGION

Overall, NDEs motivate some experiencers to become more involved in organized religion: 14 percent of our sample indicated strongly increased interest in religion, 28 percent some increase, 28 percent no change, 10 percent some decrease, and 20 percent strong decrease. In general, NDErs' greater knowledge of God and inner spirituality is not matched by greater concern with or involvement in the *outward* forms of religiosity.

NDErs develop a universalistic view of religion. One, echoing others, stated, "I came back from my experience with a much more ecumenical outlook. I am able to see the truth in all religions."

Another said, "I don't attend regularly, but when I do, I find I am comfortable with any religion or in any church."

Many NDErs do not find a major outlet for their new, intensive relationship with God in institutionalized religion. They are concerned first and foremost with promulgating the love of God they have experienced, as opposed to participating in rituals that may have little or nothing to do with love.

On the other hand, some NDErs report the experience gave them a deeper understanding of and greater appreciation for some kinds of religious rituals. Several Catholics and non-Catholics alike, told me that they had a much deeper understanding of and feeling for the Mass after their experience. One stated that since her experience, the Mass, which she had previously participated in somewhat perfunctorily, "is now like another NDE to me." A similar pattern of deeper understanding of some of the deeper meanings of her religion was apparent in another NDEr, who commented:

> Before the experience, I was a "parrot Catholic," repeating the prayers and participating in the sacraments like a parrot, without understanding the deeper meanings of the faith.

> You have to find God in the right sense. When I came back from my NDE, I went looking for the God I had experienced. I didn't know where to go so I went to the church, which I hadn't done before because I wasn't interested. It took me a long time to realize that God is not in a church; He is in people.

Mother Teresa's work with the sick, suffering, and dying of Calcutta and elsewhere rests on her firm belief that each and every person she and her associates help *is* Christ (see Spink, 1984). She looks beneath the externals of the person, including what religion he or she happens to be associated with, and relates to the Christ within. As Jesus said, "Whatever you did for the least of these my brothers of mine, you did for me" (Matthew 25:40 NIV).

This affirmation of the ultimate worth of each human being lies at the heart of the way NDErs come to view others. Although they are by no means saints, they nonetheless have been imbued with a divine love that surpasses any kind of love human beings can ordinarily experience.

BARBARA HARRIS: A JEWISH NDEr's TRANSFORMATION

Barbara's NDE occurred eight years ago when, at thirty-one, she suffered a back injury. After two years of unsuccessful treatment, she underwent a spinal fusion operation, complications from which led to her being placed in a "circle bed," a device used for spinal patients. Her NDE took place while close to death during the first week following her operation.

Like many other Jews, Barbara grew up in a family that, while nominally Jewish, did not place great emphasis on religious observance out of fear of anti-Semitism. She married a more observant Jewish man who asked her to keep a kosher home, which she refused to do because she saw herself, in her words, as a "very sophisticated young woman" and because she "refused to have anything to do with religious dogma." She did, however, concur with her husband's desire to send their three children to Hebrew school so that they would have the knowledge of their religious heritage as a basis for deciding as adults whether they wished to identify with it.

Barbara's NDE let to many changes in her life that are very similar to some basic patterns experienced by non-Jewish NDErs. Like others, she was profoundly affected by the life review aspect of her experience, developing a strong sense of self-understanding as well as a firm commitment to compassionate values. Barbara says, "The life review is where I can pinpoint all my values changing. I know beyond a reasonable doubt that my whole perception of reality changed."

Her greatly increased capacity to empathize with others led her into one of the health professions. Though notably nonreligious before the experience, she has become strongly attracted to various aspects of her religious heritage, particularly many of its rituals:

> At rituals like Rosh Hashanah, before I always used to stand back as an observer, and sometimes it repulsed me. After the NDE, I became more open-minded and observed it and respected it. And I really got into the beauty of the ritual. The Hebrew chanting just absolutely took me away. The rabbi raising the shofar, which is a ram's horn that they blow to signify the New Year—the beauty of knowing that all over the world, in every synagogue, the ram's horn is being blown to signify the New Year, it's just—I have goose pimples just telling you this.

She and another Jewish lady she knows also found much deeper meaning in traditional Jewish prayers. In particular, she cites the "Shema Y'Israel":

> Hear, O Israel, the Lord is Our God,
> The Lord is One,
> Blessed Be the Name of His Glorious Majesty
> Forever and Ever.

Of this, she states,

> "The Lord is One." That is what all my searching after the NDE has brought me to. That we are one. All of us. This prayer affirms the

unity of our oneness with God. I talked to another Jewish woman who had an NDE about a year ago. She was never that religious before either, but she told me that she now repeats the Shema to herself quite often.

However, like other NDErs, Barbara has a very universalistic outlook:

> Since my NDE, I have been brought back to all the spirituality; but I can't really say "brought back," because I never embraced religion before. And I still don't consider myself to be a religious person, if you're going to put a capital R on religion. I am a religious person for all religions, so it's a small *r*. Whatever type of organized religion I see now, I really enjoy. I really admire Catholicism—the color, the ritual. I am a human being, and my religion is being fully human. And I guess you could say that I'm very comfortable with all religions and my spiritual feelings.

Barbara has received varied reactions from other Jews with whom she has discussed her experience. She has talked with several rabbis about it, one of whom "was afraid to give an opinion. He wants to stay away from this; it makes him uncomfortable." Another rabbi told her that the only thing the Jewish religion acknowledges regarding an afterlife is that "Heaven is a place where you sit around studying Talmud. And that was it. Other than sitting and studying, there's nothing else going on. Which is pretty boring as far as I'm concerned."

However, the great Jewish theologian Martin Buber recounted a Hasidic story written by Isaac Loeb Peretz about heaven that conveys the central NDE emphasis on love and compassion. The story, entitled "If Not Higher," tells of a rabbi who, on each Day of Atonement, leaves his synagogue for several hours. Wondering if the rabbi is secretly meeting with God, one of his followers sees the rabbi don coarse clothing and enter the cottage of an elderly, infirm woman and care for her, cleaning her home and cooking. The follower returns to the synagogue and when asked by others if the rabbi had ascended to heaven, replies, "If not higher" (quoted by Hodes, 1971:52).

NDEs AND JUDEO-CHRISTIAN THEOLOGY

There are many implications of the NDE for various strands of Judeo-Christian theology. Though fuller explication is beyond the scope of this book, I will briefly summarize some of the more interesting of these implications.

In his classic work *Agape and Eros* (1932;1969) Anders Nygren distinguishes between *Eros,* human striving toward God, and *Agape,* God's unconditional love for human beings. God loves because it is His nature to do so (75), and this love is not based on the righteousness or other characteristics of those to whom it is directed. Because the overwhelming love of God NDErs experience is given to churchgoers and atheists, to "nice" people and mobsters alike, the NDE is clearly a prime manifestation of Agape because it stems neither from the efforts of NDEs to reach out toward God nor from any worthiness or lack of worthiness on their part.

The Agape NDErs experience affirms their sense of personhood because they come to know, beyond doubt, that God loves them. Moreover, this infusion of Agape gives them the capacity to look beneath the surface of others and relate to their deepest essences, and to affirm and love others unconditionally. This is clearly a prime example of the Jewish theologian Martin Buber's concept of the I-Thou relationship. An I-Thou relationship is a deep understanding of another person in which one relates to the basic divine essence of the other, as opposed to a more superficial I-It relation in which the other person is a mere means by which to achieve one's own ends. During the NDE, the experiencer comes to *know* God in an I-Thou way and thereby gains the capacity to relate to the deepest essence of others—their divine essence, or souls—in the same way. The stories of how NDErs affect others profoundly and deeply is, in Buber's terms, the epitome of the I-Thou relation in that people who are affected by NDErs' profound Agape are often able to develop a new understanding of and fellowship with God and a greater capacity for I-Thou relationships with others. Moreover, as we will show in a later chapter, the NDE can and has served as a seedbed for those who have neither had any transcendent experiences nor directly encountered NDErs to develop a greater capacity to love others in an I-Thou way rather than the "I-It" way often prescribed by social and cultural values and norms.

For some theologians and religious figures, NDE-like experiences have proven decisive. John Wesley stated that his conversion and calling stemmed from his heart's having been "strangely warmed." Similar experiences were at the root of the dynamism of such diverse figures as William Booth, founder of the Salvation Army, and C. S. Lewis, whose book *Surprised by Joy* (1955) describes the NDE-like encounter with a God of love that directed him away from his prior agnosticism.

A more directly NDE-like encounter with God provided the Princeton theologian James Loder with what he terms a "convicting experience." In a way intriguingly similar to how Tom Sawyer's NDE took place, Loder was helping a stranded elderly motorist change a tire alongside a highway when the car he was working on was struck by another from the rear. The car fell on top of Loder, and only his wife's prayer-attained miraculous strength was able to free him. Loder does not discuss many details of what he experienced, and thus it is difficult to ascertain whether his experience was an NDE or similar to one. His book *The Transforming Moment* (1981) presents a sophisticated analysis of the theological significance of convicting experiences and stresses that their genuineness, in a Christian sense, is to be gauged in the extent to which they lead to sacrificial love in the experiencer. By this criterion, the NDE clearly qualifies.

One of the most celebrated theologians of the twentieth century was a man whose major work, *The Cost of Discipleship,* was no mere abstract exercise but was put into practice in incredible strength and faith when he was imprisoned and killed by the Nazis. Despite having had many opportunities to leave his homeland, Dietrich Bonhoeffer remained in Germany during most of the thirties and was a leader in the almost entirely nonviolent resistance of a very small number of Christians to the Nazi regime. Bonhoeffer's incredible courage and strength in the face of the most severe persecution remain a strong inspiration.

One of Bonhoeffer's prime concepts is "cheap grace," the idea, prevalent in many Christian circles, that all one need do is accept God's graceful gift of forgiveness, without any subsequent need to transform one's life style and values to conform to Christ's teachings. True grace, in contrast, involves the willingness to change one's life style radically and accept even the possibility of death, as opposed to the much easier path of going to church on Sunday and being comfortably assured of forgiveness while letting the rest of one's life proceed according to the values and norms of social and cultural respectability (1963:54). Since the NDE is experienced in many cases without prior religious focus in the experiencer's life, some might consider it an instance of cheap grace. However, in addition to the obvious fact that NDErs must nearly die to attain the grace they receive, many NDErs totally transform their life styles and values, giving up material things and status to live out new lives of love. By Bonhoeffer's criteria, therefore, the divine grace experienced by NDErs is by no means cheap grace but is rather a type of grace in which the NDEr is willing to sacrifice for the sake of others, impelled by the divine imperative of love.

Finally, some of the ideas of the German theologian Wolfhart Pannenberg may prove relevant to a fuller understanding of the theological implications of the NDE. Adopting a universalistic historical perspective rooted in Old Testament revelations and Hegelian idealism, Pannenberg stresses that divine revelation is part of God's ongoing process, which will come to full culmination only at the end of time. We must, therefore, be open to the possibility of ongoing revelations that may point to the ultimate purposes of God's plan for humanity. Since a central aspect of this, according to Scripture, is triumph over death, it seems possible that the NDE might be part of God's unfolding plan pointing toward final victory over death and, therefore, freedom from the need to survive and immortality striving that is the foundation of our incapacity to fully love one another (see Olive, 1973 ff. p. 27) .

THE NDE IN
GLOBAL PERSPECTIVE

Perhaps because of the lesser availability in most (but by no means all) of the advanced biomedical technology that makes NDEs possible, there is a relative lack of reports of NDEs in non-Western societies. One of the most important new areas of research involves the investigation of NDEs in non-Western contexts. Extensive research could ascertain whether NDEs are culturally conditioned products of experiencers' subconscious or are universal.

The available evidence, though as yet limited, points to universality. The most extensive study of non-Western NDEs was undertaken by Karlis Osis and Erlendur Haraldsson. Basing their findings on reports of Indian medical personnel who were asked about NDE-like experiences of patients, Osis and Haraldsson found, in general, that the overall pattern of Indian NDEs is very similar to that of Western NDEs, with the exception that the labels the Indians attached to the Light and to other aspects of the experience were different; they were based on religious figures and imageries from their own cultural background. Thus, while the *substance* of the Indian NDEs was similar, their *interpretations* of it differed. As Osis and Haraldsson summarized an important dimension of their findings, "the finer details of otherworldly imagery seem to vary with the patient's background. Such major features as bright, saturated colors, peace, harmony, and extraordinary beauty seem, however, to prevail regardless of whether the patient is a Christian, Hindu, Jew, or Muslim" (1977:39).

Cultural and religious differences also caused somewhat different reaction patterns among Hindu Indian patients as compared with American NDErs. Noting that Americans (42 percent) had a substantially greater tendency than Indians (24 percent) toward visions of the deceased with feelings of serenity and peace, Osis and Haraldsson state, "The difference is understandable in light of Indian mythology. As explained before, Yama, the god of death, has messengers (Yamdoots) whose appearance may depend upon the moral quality of the dying person's life. They are often portrayed in a rather sinister fashion. When such Yamdoots are encountered, one would not wonder over any display of negative emotion" (1977:110).

However, they emphasize that both Indian and American NDEs are accompanied by a preponderance of overwhelmingly positive reactions related to the common centrality of love and compassion at the heart of the highest ideals of both traditions:

> Hinduism, at its best, is a highly developed religion that propagates love and self-transcendence. But the dark side of the Hindu religion—portrayed by Yama, Yamdoots, and various demons— comprises about one-fifth of the religious figures seen by Indian patients. Positive emotions seem to accompany apparitions of such deities as Krishna, Shiva, or other benevolent celestial beings (for example, the devas).

> It is, of course, universal that a certain kind of negative emotion is associated with religion. The Bible speaks about the fear of God quite often in the Old Testament, but Christianity, characteristically enough, has deemphasized these negative aspects. One does not find an expression such as "the fear of Christ" in the New Testament. This Christian emphasis on positive religious emotions might also be the reason for the differences in emotional reactions of American and Indian patients to religious figures. However, there are more similarities than differences. In spite of very different cultural conditioning, many patients in both countries showed

the same emotional reaction. That is, Hindus "light up" as Americans do. (1977:110–111)

In *Heading toward Omega,* Kenneth Ring summarizes some possible implications of the NDE for Eastern religions. All major world religions strive to overcome ties to the transitory things of the world and to attain unity with the Ultimate, however it is conceived. Ring shows the relevance of such phenomena as the Kundalini experience to the NDE and shows that many sages of Eastern religious traditions have had NDE-like experiences.

Unfortunately, there are no data of which I am aware of the kinds of effects the experience has on the values, outlooks, and lives of Hindu (or, for that matter, other non-Western) peoples. In lieu of such research, the best that can be done at this point is to point out certain kinds of fundamental congruencies between some of the central belief and value orientations of non-Western religious traditions and the kinds of changes we have seen as promulgated by the NDE among Western experiencers.

There are clear parallels between certain Hindu beliefs and value orientations and the kinds of changes NDEs undergo. Perhaps the most striking of these is the congruence between the Hindu emphasis on nonviolence and respect for life and similar attitudes characteristic of NDErs. Moreover, the Hindu conception of the ultimate goal of human existence through successive incarnations as uniting with Brahma, the Absolute, is in general suggestive of the NDErs' encounter with the Being of Light, although again careful research would be necessary to specify the exact kinds of possible parallels that may exist between various aspects of Hindu religion and mysticism and the NDE.

With respect to Buddhism, a number of congruencies also seem apparent. Buddhism began with the young Prince Gautama leaving his palace and family and going out into the world to witness the suffering, pain, and death of the mass of humanity he had been sheltered from. Moved by compassion, he meditated for several years and gained enlightenment. Central to his insight was the idea that desire is the basis of suffering and that the answer to suffering lies in the recognition that there is no separate ego, that we are all part of a whole.

Generally speaking, this seems quite similar to the kind of insight NDErs gain. In particular, it seems very congruent with NDErs' new perspective that the self we consider basic to our existence is just a "bubble" that is replaced by becoming part of the universe and the rest of humanity as one consequence of death. Moreover, the fact that the young Buddha's quest for enlightenment was initiated by his empathic compassion for the sufferings he witnessed is highly congruent with NDErs' newfound compassion and empathy for others and their desire to do things for others. Thus, the Buddhist emphasis on selfish desire as the basis of suffering and its adherents' attempts to overcome desire and arrive at a state of enlightenment, culminating in a state of nirvana, seems, in an overall sense, congruent with the NDErs' belief that, as one put it, they have reached "a state we all want to attain but never quite are able to."

Moreover, Professor Carl Becker, a specialist in Eastern religion and philosophy, has suggested (1981) that NDErs' conceptions of the afterlife are similar to various aspects of Buddhist thought and practice. Various others have noted the close similarities between the experiences of the afterlife in the Tibetan Book of the Dead and many aspects of the NDE.

Likewise, there appear to be certain similarities between the values and beliefs of Islam and the NDE. The sense of brotherhood of all believers and the relative simplicity and racial and other tolerance of the Islamic community resonates with similar patterns reported by NDErs. Throughout the Koran, Allah, the compassionate, the merciful, emphasizes the importance of helping the poor, the widowed, and orphans and of avoiding selfishness. These are also central messages conveyed by the Light to NDErs.

Though, again, much research is needed, and more non-Western NDEr accounts must become available to scholars for analysis, it seems that the NDE may provide a validation of certain common threads that run through most, if not all, major world religions and many minor ones. In particular, each seems to include as a central value orientation and belief a strong concern for others in the form of, among other elements, some version of the Golden Rule. This basic belief in the supreme importance of caring for others is the most striking affirmation that NDErs report as the most significant aspect of the experience. NDErs are able to see the elements of truth in every religion and adopt a universalistic rather than dogmatic approach. Barbara Harris expresses a message of the NDE that is central to all religions:

> A beautiful poetic way of looking at it is that when you're on the right path, when you're on the right road, when you're enlightened, whatever, just picture driving your car down this beautiful

path that's all wooded, big beautiful trees, and straight ahead of you is the sun. It's so magnificent that it's blinding. So you really can't see where you're going, but you know you're headed straight for it. You can see how beautiful the trip is, you can look on either side of you and see the trees, and know that you're on a beautiful journey. That's how I feel my life is going now. It's this beautiful journey, with this bright light ahead of me.

Universal
Christ

A central issue for Christians with regard to the NDE is, How does it relate to their faith? In particular, does it confirm or deny their faith in Jesus Christ as the Son of God who is the only basis of salvation?

Numerous books have been written about the NDE from the Christian perspective. With few exceptions, most tend to adopt the view that the NDE is some sort of demonic deception, as indicated in 2 Corinthians 11:14, in which the Apostle Paul states the devil can disguise himself as an "angel of light."

As I will try to show here, the NDE affirms the uniqueness and centrality and indispensability of Christ, *but in a universalistic way that does not negate or diminish the value of other religious traditions.* First, many overlook the fact that the book that "started it all," Raymond Moody's *Life after Life,* is *dedicated to Christ*: The "One" the dedication refers to *is* Christ, to whom George Ritchie, the devout Christian who had the original NDE that piqued Raymond's interest in the subject, suggested Moody dedicate the book. This is because Ritchie's experience, which occurred in 1943 when he was a young man in the Army and was clinically dead of pneumonia, was very Christ-centered: It was *Jesus* who took Ritchie around and showed him the various realms of heaven, as well as the "earth-bound spirits" who were hellishly suffering the consequences of their selfishness, materialism, and other negative orientations (see Ritchie and Sherrill, 1973).

Other NDEs have been reported with a very Christ-centered orientation. Nina Helene, for a doctoral dissertation, studied and reported on over two dozen cases of individuals who saw Christ and received other messages of a specifically Christian content, and afterward not only found their faith strengthened but also in many instances experienced newfound healing and other powers (1984).

The crucial question, however, for Christians is: Is an NDE that does *not* explicitly have Jesus in it still a genuine encounter with God? Or is it, as some have put it, a "spiritual counterfeit"?

This issue is so central and important that I am devoting a whole chapter to it. I am convinced that the NDE has the potential of revitalizing and affirming commitment to the teachings of Christ and to Jesus, but in a universal way that can and will break through sectarian and other barriers and shine a laser beam of Light on the true essence and meaning of Christ for *all* people.

This chapter will begin by examining some ways in which Christians have reacted to the NDE in terms of their formal religious commitments. I will then present an extensive discussion of negative experiences, a topic of great concern to Christians who believe NDEs present nothing but positive conceptions of the afterlife. Then I will quote an extensive dialogue I undertook with Tom Sawyer in an effort to resolve the crucial question of the relationship between Christ and the Light. As this shows, the Light *is* Christ, the *universal* Christ transcending all imageries and all ideologies and bringing all people together at a time when humanity desperately needs salvation from the nuclear devastation that threatens not only Christians but people of all religions as well as those of no faith. At such a time, it seems reasonable that a loving God and Christ would be trying to "get through" with the message of love, of the unconditional grace in the pure Light of Agape, that is at the heart of the NDE.

CHURCH INVOLVEMENT

To many people, being a "Christian" means being involved in a church or in some form of organized religion. How do NDEs stack up on this score?

A Catholic NDEr originally had difficulty integrating the experience. She told me she kept trying to find in church the love she had experienced during the NDE but couldn't do so. Despite this initial difficulty, she eventually found a more love-oriented (as opposed to ritualistic and legalistic) Catholic parish and has become very active in it, getting a great deal of pleasure and meaning out of singing in the choir and other activities. Similarly, several Catholics have said they became much more involved in their church after their experiences.

A Protestant NDEr found her faith deepened and strengthened by an NDE that took place as a result of a mountain-climbing accident:

> I am known as one of the most enthusiastic of Christians. *Enthusiastic* was the word used *before* my experience. The enthusiasm before was outward and since has drawn inward into a yearning to be *real* and to be the me I was created to be in yielding my own life up to preferring others before myself. Before, I wanted the world to *see* and help me and admire the beautiful walk with God I had. Now I want to love people with the love God loved me as the Light of His love ebbed through me as I dissolved in it for a moment of life-changing revelation. That love does not exploit nor call attention to itself.

Since her experience, she places greater emphasis on helping others on a one-to-one basis rather than trying to convert them. This attitude is also reflected in the comments of Nancy Clark:

> I don't feel a strong need to be evangelical about the work that I do. I don't feel a need to convert people in a religious sense. I feel I'm very, extremely, low-key in this respect. I do feel that this sense of divine love within me speaks for Himself, and I believe that people can sense the genuineness of my deep spirituality and I think that this speaks louder than words.

Among Protestant as well as Catholic NDErs, Mother Teresa of Calcutta is often cited as exemplifying the promulgation of God's love. As one NDEr put it:

> Mother Teresa. *That's* Christianity. Or Father Ritter of Times Square, who helps homeless kids. Mother Teresa *is* and *does* what she *says*. Total giving. I don't know if I could do what she has done. How many years did she go about doing her work before anybody heard of her? How many lives did she touch every day? It's the unselfish love and caring that's important. And look at it this way: If everyone did just a little, she wouldn't have to do so much.

NEGATIVE EXPERIENCES, JUDGMENT, AND HELL

One of the most common questions asked of researchers dealing with the NDE as well as NDErs themselves is, "What about negative experiences?" The overwhelming majority of NDErs researchers have interviewed have had generally positive experiences.

The assumption that the NDE presents a totally positive picture of death with no element of judgment is, however, simply incorrect. Elaine Winner, who has given many talks before religious groups concerned with this issue, relates that as she was going through the tunnel she saw a realm of "troubled spirits":

> It's a dusky, dark, dreary area, and you realize that the area is filled with a lot of lost souls, or beings, that could go the same way I'm going [to the Light] if they would just look up. The feeling I got was that they were all looking downward, and they were kind of

shuffling, and there was a kind of moaning. There were hundreds of them, looking very dejected. The amount of confusion I felt coming off of it was tremendous. When I went through this, I felt there was a lot of pain, a lot of confusion, a lot of fear, all meshed into one. It was a very heavy feeling. They weren't turning toward the Light. In fact, they didn't even know the Light existed.

So many times, fundamentalists think the NDE takes away from the judgmental aspect depicted in the Bible. But when you go into this Light, you realize the injustices that you as a person have created in the lives of other people. For me, it was *feeling* those injustices. I *felt* the pain I had caused. You *feel* your iniquities, your shortcomings. You feel it all. You feel yourself judged. But at the same time, you feel loved and forgiven.

The questions also come up about whether or not the NDE does away with the consequences of living a bad life: criminals, that type of person. Going in that Light is a beautiful feeling in that you feel love and forgiveness. To not be able to stay in that realm of heavenly love would *be* hell. To experience it, to know that it's there, and not be able to partake of it: That's hell.

Every experiencer tells me the same thing I felt and experienced. Not all of them *saw* anything, but they *felt* it.

AN NDEr's CLINICAL IMPRESSION
OF NEGATIVE EXPERIENCES

Professor Kimberly Clark has pioneered in the application of clinical social work methods in helping NDErs cope with their experiences. She has interviewed hundreds of experiencers, and is herself an NDEr. At a conference at Miami University she offered her clinical impressions of negative experiences. She stresses that the observations and generalizations she makes are not based on systematic research. Nonetheless, her wide professional experience with NDErs makes her impressions useful as preliminary indications of general patterns that may prove characteristic of negative experiences when extensive research is undertaken.

Based on what I have perceived, and I'm not the only person who can talk this way, there is an opposite to all the loving, good, Godlike things that is very negative, very scary. I perceive evil as a separate entity, just a I perceive love as a separate entity, based on my personal experience. I'm not saying, "Yes there is, No there isn't", just based on my experience, or rather experiences, in the multiples, great multiples. I see evil as a separate and very powerful entity. It gets at my ego, and my ego is like a zoo animal—Feed me! (laughs).

People who have negative experiences are afraid of death. Not forever, but for a long time. Can you blame them? There's lots of problems with a negative experience. It's hard enough to talk about a positive experience. I think there are a lot more negative experiences than people talk about. In his 1982 poll Gallup said that 1 percent of NDErs have negative experiences. I see more than that. I think there's many more than 1 percent. I don't think they've done what I'd call adequate research to determine how much more then 1 percent. I think I hear increasingly more negative experiences because I'm talking about them. I do a lot of television shows and research and lectures like this. It takes about four months for people to open up and talk about negative experiences. People will call and begin to talk about them, but then change their mind and say, "Goodbye, I have to go." And they often won't tell you who they are when they call.

With someone who's had a positive experience, it takes about three or four attempts. With someone who's had a negative experience, it takes twice as long. To date, everyone I've talked to who's told me about their negative experience has given me their name, but sometimes I won't hear from them ever again after they related it to me.

There are some common threads that I have found, based on my clinical experiences. There are people who have demonic visions, and feel that they are physically and/or emotionally prompted by evil entities, scary little demons: these are the words people use, you know, "demonic beings." One experiencer who had such an experience was told very convincingly by all of these demons that her life was a sham, that it wasn't real.

Well, I agree with that, because what I was experiencing in my NDE was far more real than this (life). This is a shallow experience. We have five senses and stuff, and we feel that this is life and that this is great. But in an NDE, good or bad, it's ultra-dimensional. This was impossible for me to convey until about two months ago when I was looking at a comic strip and it occurred to me that comics are two-dimensional, and this is like trying to tell the world of the people on a comic page what life is all about, like all the Peanuts gang, or anyone on a comic page who is on a comic page and living in two dimensions what it's like to be in a three-dimensional world where there's depth, and where you can see, and hear, and smell, and touch. How would Blondie understand?

Well, it's like that in an NDE. There are lots of dimensions. Now, if it's a negative experience, it still has that ultra-dimensional quality. It's more real than real. So in my friend's (negative) experience there were these beings telling her that her life was a sham, that the major (demonic) being had made it all up, that it was like she was an actress on a stage, and that she belonged to him, and that she was bad. It was awful for her to tell about her experience. It was just terrifying. She sat on that information for twenty-five years, which is a long time to suffer.

Another kind of negative experience, the worst kind of negative experience I ever heard of, is the absolute opposite of the positive experience. People find themselves in a tunnel. Then the Light appears, this Light, I can't tell you how magnetic it is. If you could combine all the love that you've ever felt for anybody, and think of all the people that you are now separated from because of death or whatever—your children, your lovers, all your former lovers, your parents, your teachers, anybody that you're right now not with, and think about how you might long to see them, and magnify that millions of times. The absolute magnetic quality of that Light: there's that kind of longing when you see it.

But then, the worst experience would be to be pulled away from it. There are people I've talked to who have had that experience. I think it would be the worst experience. As one person described it, it's like those old televisions when you'd turn off the set and there'd be this little flash of light and it would get smaller and smaller. Well, that's how people would describe their experience. The Light would get smaller and smaller, and yet they'd be longing for it. Not only that, but knowing that they'd face an absolute extinction of the soul.

All the people I know who have had negative experiences have become Bible-based Christians. And that's interesting to me. I'm not saying that all people who have negative experiences become that way, but all the ones I know have become Bible-based. They might express it in various sects. But they all feel that they have come back from an awful situation and have a second chance.

One of the first people I ever interviewed had been an S.O.B. before his negative experience. He beat his wife and kids and drank himself into the ground. When I encountered his wife and children, I was all set for a big grief reaction, when it looked like he wouldn't make it. But she was so happy that he was dying. And when the kids came in, they all went, Oh, thank goodness, we thought he was never going to die! (laughs). Well, as it turns out, he didn't die, and he changed completely. He now makes toys for children and devotes his time to helping others. He's a wonderful person—warm, loving, a great person. His wife divorced him. It turns out she didn't like the new Mr. _____. It's very complex, but she needed (his previous ways) in her life as much as she hated it.

As Professor Clark indicates, the lack of emphasis on negative experiences in most books about NDEs is not necessarily an indication of their rarity, but of the difficulty in discussing them that negative NDErs understandably encounter. A number of books have been written by writers whose fundamentalist orientations have led them to include that NDEs are demonic deceptions of the type warned against by the Apostle Paul in Second Corinthians 11:14. Tim LaHaye (1980), Phillip Swihart (1978) and others maintain that the apparent lack of negative, "hellish" experiences in Moody's and other accounts indicates that the NDE presents a view in which punishment is absent and that for anyone, no matter what kind of life he or she leads or whatever his or her relationship to Christ, there is no judgment. In the most extensive work thus far published that focuses on negative experiences, cardiologist Maurice Rawlings (1978) discusses several observations of negative NDEs that came to his attention. In some, patients, during resuscitation efforts, would cry out that they were in hell, and not remember anything about their experience when revived. In others, Rawling's experiences reported being in the characteristic, classical Hell of fire and brimstone, crying out to Jesus to save them, and being brought back. All became fervent believers in Christ.

Though substantial numbers of accounts of negative experiences, not to mention quantitative data, are definitely lacking in the study of negative experiences, and much research needs to be done, it seems a safe generalization that there is a strong relationship between such experiences and religious faith. Though cross-cultural studies need to be done, it seems that negative experiences have a strong tendency to serve as what theologian James Loder (1981) terms "convicting experiences." Negative NDEs seem to function much like conversion experiences in some respects, in that they demonstrate to a person the need to change his/her orientations in life and point out the saving grace that can be found in a belief in Christ.

JENNY: AN NDE-LIKE
CONVERSION EXPERIENCE

A student in one of my classes, after hearing Nancy Clark talk about her experience, approached me and told me that she had had a similar experience that changed her life. While it is unclear the extent to which her experience involved clinical death, it has many of the same aspects as the kind of negative NDEs discussed by Kimberly Clark, and had the same consequence—a new-found committment to Christianity.

One day, while riding around with a friend, my student, who I'll call Jenny, took some drugs and began to experience strong reactions. Her friend, scared about what was happening, kept on driving, and finally took Jenny to a hospital. But during the time of what seemed to her friend both convulsions and a death-like condition that followed, Jenny had an NDE-like experience that changed her life totally. As Jenny describes it:

> We were in a park, and it was late at night. We smoked the pot, and then we started walking back to the car. We were laughing and stuff. Then all of a sudden it was like deja vu, and I said "Listen, Beth, we've been here before, haven't we?" Then I got in the car, and she started driving, and she was only going about 25 miles an hour. I kept screaming, "You've got to be going seventy miles an hour. We're going to get arrested."

> Then I started going real crazy, and she strapped me into the car, and it was in wintertime, so she threw snow down my shirt to try to calm me down, and I felt like I was on fire, I was just screaming. That was when my eyes closed. She just started driving around, because she didn't know what to do. She thought I was dead.

> At this time, my spiritual self left my body. I could see everything, I could tell her everything—where she drove, everything. Like when she drove through this shopping center, I could tell her what these people were wearing.

> Then, I felt like I was moving down. It felt like a train, and I was moving down to Hell. It was all dark, it was just real painful. It was both emotional and physical, more physical. It was was like a gut feeling that just emanated throughout my whole body and I knew this wasn't a nice place to be. And I kept going, Dear God, if you let me live again, then I'll do what you want me to do.

> Before this, I had gone to church, but it was simply because mother had gotten me dressed on Sunday mornings and took me. But to

me, it was nothing. I had been to Sunday school, but I never listened, I never cared. It wasn't important to me.

Then, when I had spoken and said "Please let me live," I started moving away from the darkness towards the Light. It was sort of like a tradeoff. If I would start living my life like a Christian, and maybe showing other people what Christianity is all about, then He would let me live. And so, at about that time, when I was in the hospital, I started coming back out of it.

During the negative part of the experience, there was just darkness, and I was all alone. I didn't see any figures the whole time. It was a feeling, just the emotional aspect of it. It was desolate, it was awful. And I kept thinking "All I want to do is get out of here. How can I do it?" And that was when I saw the Light. And I had to keep moving toward it.

I felt like the Devil wanted me down there, and I had to fight my way to get to the Light. I realized what I wanted in my life and where I was going, and that it wasn't the right way. The Light showed me what I could look forward to after I died. It showed me a lot of things in this world that aren't good. A lot of things need to be changed.

I gained a lot of understanding. I saw that we're moving so fast in our society, we're not taking time to look at what God has given us. We're not getting to know people, which is the essence of what it's all about. We're not here to be making millions of dollars and getting to the top of the corporate ladder. That's not what God wants us to do. We're here for people.

After the experience, I at first didn't realize what it all meant. I sort of tried to put it away, suppress it in some way, because I was so scared of it. I didn't know what had happened to me. And then, for some reason, things just started coming back to me, little incidents, and I started wondering what it really was. I couldn't go to school, I was so scared, I told my father I didn't understand what was going on in my mind. Then I went to see a psychiatrist, and he just let me talk about it. And through that, I was able to understand it more. He wasn't a real believer in Christ or anything, and he didn't talk about that, but I have a real good friend who is, and I talked to her about it too, and she said it was a real definite message from God. And I started reading the Bible more and more and I started realizing, Yes, that's what it was.

I started going to Bible Study. It wasn't something I had to do, it was something I wanted to do because I wanted to learn more about it.

I think the experience was a gift from God to me. Parts of it I would like to experience again, like the part with God, but the beginning part I would never like to experience again. That was very scary, something that nobody would want to experience.

My whole outlook on life has changed. Before, I was very self-centered, everything was me, me, me. And now, I give more to other people. I show love more. I have a spiritual relationship with God which builds my character. And my goals in life have become stronger. I've seen both sides, and I look at people and wonder, why? The way they treat other people, the way they're so self-centered. I look at them the way they used to be. I feel sorry for them.

As far as church goes, I work on Sundays so I don't go to church here. See, I don't think that going to church is important, I think that it's important to spend time with God each and every day. By yourself. Reading the Bible, praying, having your quiet time every day. That's what's important. A one-on-one relationship with Christ through God.

I'm much better able to understand other people now. I find myself more tolerant, I look at different sides of an issue, I realize that in every situation there are two stories and to simply look at it in one way is wrong. Now, people come to me and I help them with problems. Before, I don't think anybody would come to me and tell me anything, problemwise, or ask for assistance, but now I'm more willing and understanding and more better able to help them.

Before the experience, I had no career plans. I wasn't even sure I was going to go to college. I was sixteen at the time, and now I'm nineteen. But now, I want to be in a job working with people, not as a social worker, but maybe in a corporation working with union and non-union contracts, labor. Getting people to have an agreement. Trying to help people come together.

During the experience, I didn't really have any life review, but just the feeling that where I was going and how I had lived my life until then was wrong, and that the end result would be what I experienced before seeing the Light. And I realized that wasn't what I wanted at all. It was a void. You were void of any feelings. It was awful.

In the strict sense, of course, Jenny's experience was not an NDE but rather more like a conversion experience. Nonetheless, at the time she had had substantial experiences with drugs and stated that her NDE-like encounter was nothing like a drug-induced experience. In her words,

> This was on a different level than any drug-induced state. I feel pretty lucky, because I know what I'm going towards, and it's something good and it's something positive. And out of all the badness that I had from this experience, so much more positive has come out of it for me. In listening to Nancy Clark, I could understand the feelings that she was trying to convey. But I didn't have a huge Light envelop me, I just went towards the Light.

In sum, it is clear that however they occur, negative experiences have a profound impact on people and lead to substantial transformations, particularly in the more traditional sense of religious conversion.

CHRIST AND THE LIGHT

NDErs also frequently encounter those who feel their experience is somehow a denial of the centrality of Christ, or even a demonic deception. Several books have been written setting forth this view.

I have talked with a number of NDErs about this, and they all say that they see themselves as carrying out God's imperative of love for Him and others. Elaine Winner tells of a typical interaction with a concerned Christian:

> The question a fundamentalist asked me was, "Was this [the Light] a God figure, was it a Christ figure, or was it an angelic being?" And I told him, first of all, "I'd like to know what the difference is between God and Christ." And he said that the Bible talks about God and about Christ, and that Christ was the physical man, the Son of God, and I told him that it also says in the Bible, in Christ's teaching, "If you have seen Me, you have seen the Father." And I mentioned that the Light has to be God because I couldn't imagine that kind of powerful energy in an angel. And I didn't think an angel could cause us to feel the pain of the injustices that we create. He accepted this. At least, there were no more questions from him.

Others are often very impressed with the changes NDErs exhibit after their experiences. One NDEr said, "I have a very dear friend who is a typical, loving, kind, beautiful born-again Christian. I'm consoled by the fact that she has known me both before and after my experience, and knows of my honesty, and she's seen the changes."

NDErs' lack of emphasis on belief, doctrine, and dogma and on theologizing as a whole reflects their focus on the God of unconditional, total love and knowledge they encountered during their experiences, and from whom they learned that the purpose of life is to promulgate this love by allowing themselves to be used as instruments of the Light. As Nancy Clark puts it:

> I do not feel the need to debate theological differences with anyone. I find that people get so focused on the *religiosity* of God that they approach their own spirituality a little like "tunnel vision." A Baptist minister once told me that my experience, and consequently my interest in promulgating these experiences, was the work of the devil. Can you believe that? He was so focused on his religiosity that he failed to see this experience as the catalyst to a deeper and more profound spirituality in which God Himself becomes the focus of one's life. This is what I mean when I accuse some deeply religious people of having "tunnel vision." They are not able to see, really, the entire picture. They're so focused, perhaps, on their rules and regulations and belief concepts and traditions that they can't see the God of love.

> With regard to the kind of divine experience I had, if it doesn't conform to someone's religious beliefs or church doctrines, and so forth, then they're extremely reluctant to believe those of us who have genuinely encountered our Heavenly Father. When we try to relate our transformative experiences to them, somehow we're seen as a threat to them and to their religious convictions. How sad that is! I feel it is very important for me to try to bridge this gap between us by helping those who feel this way to get a broader understanding of God through the spirituality that He manifests within me, and among the countless others who have undergone a similar experience. I believe we have a great gift to share with all the religions of the world, if only they will listen and not feel threatened by us.

UNIVERSAL GRACE

The NDE is a gift of *universal* grace that nonexperiencers, as Tom Sawyer emphasizes, can share in. He suggests one way to do this:

With the amount of knowledge the reader has regarding his or her religion, his or her culture, and all those things, sit down and be still, even while reading the book, as you're ready to turn to the next page, hesitate for four or five minutes and try to think of nothing, which is basically impossible for a first-timer. You know, most humans can't think of nothing. It's an extraordinary accomplishment if a person can ever do that. But be still, and try to observe your overall life up to that point in time. In other words, pretend to do a life review, or have a life review.

The first time you do that, you'll be judgmental about many of the good things you did. That's kind of hard to handle for the first time.

And then later in the book, after they've read about more things, more aspects of the NDE and its implications, suggest that they do the same thing, only this time, review the good things and the bad things, only don't judge them. Don't say, "Oh, gee, that's bad," and "Wow, neat, it's good." Just know they were learning experiences, a combination of good and bad. And then try to perceive that regardless of what has been done in the past, every individual has the opportunity to now start striving toward unconditional love, which starts with unconditional love of the self. And if you can unconditionally forgive yourself, once you've decided you've done things that are judgmentally negative and bad, totally forgive yourself for that. Don't worry about excuses.

I asked him, "Doesn't Christ come in here?"

Well, sure! That's who Christ is! That's *what* Christ is! To take the punishment for those things, so that you are no longer judged by them. Right! And because of our iniquities, and the human condition, we require, or have required, the Christ figure—Christ the man and Christ the figure. And the essence of Jesus Christ, which still exists. In other words, as a stepping stone toward experiencing joy and the Light of Jesus, experiencing that Light, that unconditional love, and all those things life should be and *can* be, has the ability to be. And use Him that way. That's what He's there for.

Historically, the function had to be to have the man, in other words, in the form of a man, because humankind lost the pure, unadulterated perception of the Christ. I mean, there had been too many images built on images built on images, and mixed in there with greed and ego, it got to the point where things weren't pure enough for the average individual to break through that imagery and those prejudices and see love. And it boiled down to the big word, in capital letters, *LOVE.* Christ broke through those images. It was necessary for Him to say and show and do and *be* unconditional love.

Does this mean that heaven is populated only by "card-carrying Christians," as theologian Paul Knitter (1985) puts it?

In a dialogue Tom and I carried on about the Christian implications of the NDE, I asked him:

> There is this crucial issue about the indispensability of Christ—that "No one comes to the Father but through Me"—and the NDE seems to say, you can come to the Father through an NDE; therefore, you don't need Christ.

Tom replied:

> Well, I disagree with that. I disagree with that. And it may be just a play on words or a matter of perception, but as far as I'm concerned, the Light—the approach of the Light, the tunnel situation (and here we go again with imagery)—*what is it that you're basking in?* I mean if *that is not 100 percent the Light of Christ*—it can't be anything else.

"The fundamentalists say it's Satan—the angel of light referred to in 2 Corinthians 11:14."

> I've learned that since the experience. Terrific. So let's go past Satan. Theoretically, or basically speaking, what's the job of the devil, or Satan?

"To keep us away from heaven."

> All right, now what I'm really going to ask myself, and ask you, is: Is this what I'm doing?

"You don't need to convince me."

> I know that. But just for my sake, in other words as a demonstration of who's right and who's wrong, a theoretical argument with one of these people. Okay, fine. I say that that was the Light of Jesus. And I say that the Light was God. And now that I'm here, through no fault of my own—trust me on that—through no fault

of my own; I made the right decision, I didn't want to come back here, I wanted to stay. But through whatever service or reason or whatever, I'm here now. So does that mean that I've been exposed to the Light of Satan? And are the things that I do—I mean, maybe because I swear now and then, maybe I am Satan. In other words, what I do by going to Mass and having these *extraordinary* ecstatic experiences, the things that I do talking and loving people toward unconditionally, because that's such a high order.

"The fundamentalists would ask, "Have you accepted Jesus as your personal Savior?" Because the Bible says you must accept Jesus Christ as your personal Savior in order to gain eternal life, and only if you have done that can you be saved."

Right. See, again, because I'm a stickler for detail, in that the only problem with that is, in *their* perception, are they saying, Jesus Christ *the man,* or are they saying *the Christ?*

"The Christ. Sure."

Oh, all right! If they're saying "the Christ," then *yes!* Then absolutely yes to all of that. And then the only thing I'm not doing is using a minimum of 15 percent of my income for their church, and stuff like that.

"What they would say is, 'Are you trying to lead people to Christ, so they can be saved?"'

In effect, yes. However, maybe I don't qualify for that, because I can see, I can know, that a Buddhist who has never spelled the word *Christ* or *Jesus* will get to the Christ Light even if it means through an entire lifetime, and upon his transformation, or from the point of clinical death to actual death or whatever it is—he may take that long—and only at such time will he then see the difference between Buddha and Christ—and *the* Christ. But at that time, he will be *in* the Christ Light, so it's all redundant. It's all irrelevant, at the moment in time for that person. And It'll be a success. It'll be there.

"What *is* the difference between Buddha, and other religious leaders, and Christ?"

Buddha was a *man,* a man who had a tremendous spiritual awakening. He came to *know* and *see* the Light. But he was not *of* it directly. Jesus was unique in how He came to be incarnated by typical parents and lived a typical childhood. Jesus was incarnated, for sure, by divine intervention.

Now [after the NDE], I am a Christian [he was an agnostic previously]. Yes, there is something unique about Jesus. Very basically, He, in measured or known history, is the only entity born to be the Christ. He is the only entity to come directly from the Light all the way down through the stages—from the Light directly to the earth plane.

"Evangelicals and many other Christians say that what happens when you die, you, in effect, confront God, and with your sins the way they are and so forth, your "grossness" or whatever you want to call it, is simply unacceptable to God. I mean, you can't become part of the Light."

Right.

"All right, by accepting Christ, what happens is that Christ has paid the price for your sins and therefore you are judged not on the basis of those sins; in other words, He stands in your stead. So God accepts Christ rather than you, and you are then able to become part of the Light or enter heaven or whatever."

Right. And, of those people who die and end up in a purgatory or a hellish situation, it's just exactly that. They either can't comprehend or can't accept Christ at that point, and therefore have to be overeducated or reeducated, so to speak, or given time to have the proper perception or that cleansing or that whatever, to the point at which they *will* accept the Christ, and be in a pure enough state, or cleansed or all of that stuff, to then blend right into the Light.

"But what Christianity also says is that none of us will *ourselves* be pure enough."

Right. In bodily form. But that ends at clinical death. You notice, I said *at* clinical death. Because at clinical death, there is *such* a separation of the physical body to the spiritual.

"Christians would say that some of us can become purified enough through our own efforts."

> No, not 100 percent. But God help you if you're only 20 percent there, compared with everyone else who may be 80 percent there. Because you're going to be in a hellish situation to make up for that extra 60 percent.

"On the other hand, Christ can make up—make it 100 percent."

> Right. And the problem there is, people greedily or egotistically or selfishly rely on Christ the man, or Christ the thing that you pray to, or the Christ Light itself, to do their work for them, whether it's as a *substitute* for what you know intuitively that you are supposed to be doing or that you must or have to do—many people *don't* do, and they use that as their "ace in the hole" or their calling card: "Well, not to worry, 'cause Christ will do it for me, or take care of it for me." In other words, Christ will be the whipping boy.

"But that would be contradictory to Christians' doctrine of Christ. In other words, by accepting Christ, a murderer or some other person who has done evil—his or her sins are washed away, and he or she can enter heaven."

> That's true.

"So then Christ is the Savior."

> That's true. In other words, here's where our perception of justice fails us.

"I know. But that's the whole point, of divine grace. Because no matter what you do, no matter how undeserving you are . . ."

> Right.

"Amazing grace . . . "

> That murderer has performed murder, and can be cleaned in the matter of a second. And me, simply being a speeder, in other words, I got speeding tickets, I may take a couple of years. And that's the

difference between individuality. Even with those at a rather high spiritual level, there's still individuality.

"Now wait. The Christian says that God wants us to be united with Him in heaven. So therefore, Christ was provided as a means whereby even those people who were totally gross and wacked out and all that, by accepting Christ, can gain that unity."

Right. And it allows for . . .

"But not through our own efforts. In other words, the point is that we can do nothing. It's divine grace. Now, is that congruent [with what you learned during the NDE]? In other words, it's God's gift to us without us deserving anything because of our own efforts."

Right. In other words, Mother Teresa is *not* guaranteed a free pass—in other words, an express pass.

"Through her good works?"

Right.

"Why not?"

Because there's no justice in nature. In other words, the justice breaks down. Our measurement is that she's better than you and I because she spends more hours and a greater physical effort and emotional effort. . . .

"But the divine justice breaks down because of grace, right?"

Yes. I'm saying, in *our* judgments, Mother Teresa is not *necessarily* qualified. But the probability is that she is.

"But there is that element of divine grace. . . . Let's say, all right, Attica [Prison]. Now, some preacher goes there and says, "Look, you want to go to Heaven, accept Christ." And the guy says, "Yes," and he cries and goes through the born-again conversion process. Then he later dies, and he goes through the tunnel, and he's entered into the Light despite being a murderer and everything. All right?"

Right. Now he will have the life review, and *that's* where things can either pass right on through, on an express pass, or things can stop suddenly and change and get distorted.

"All right, let's take criminal number two, who hasn't accepted Christ: 'Ah, I don't need this!'' '

Well, he ain't gonna get it. And he may or may not either come back to life, in other words, in a real death situation, and that will either continue and continue and continue until such time as I can be either cleansed or whatever.

"But by accepting Christ in the full, real sense, as our personal Savior, means that whatever you've done or not done on the basis of your own efforts or whatever you can be united with the Light?"

You have the *purest,* born-again Christian, the one who during his or her lifetime is born again, *fervently* believes in Jesus Christ as his or her Savior, all of this stuff, goes to church, does all kinds of servitude-type things, is all-around All-American, or All-World, good guy. Okay? He or she may *still* not be pure enough and he or she may have perceptions that he or she must perceive. The perception is there that even if you're a model *A* student, you may not have taken all the courses and paid attention well enough. The record is there—straight *A*'s—but is the *essence* there, is the *substance* there? Are the learning *experiences* there? See, you've got the scholastic proof, you've got the record, in other words, you've read all the books, but have you *experienced* all that you have to know? So here we have a born-again Christian who is so pure, so divine, and so saintly, and then dies and makes a transformation, and *still* does not have an express pass. But again, we're kind of zeroing in on exceptional cases. He or she can't attain a situation of 100 percent unconditional love in the human condition because of all the things that make up the human condition.

"Would Christ provide him with that express pass?"

Right. The stronger probability is that there would be that. Even though they use the Bible to say a lot of things it doesn't mean to say, the basic thing they're selling or telling or believing is that you have to accept the Christ Light—the Christ—as your Savior to gain entry to the pure Light of God—the Whole, the One.

"Now, is that true?"

> *Yes!* Yes! And it holds true for every single human being that has
> been on the earth, B.C. and A.D.

"One of things that has helped me a lot was a minister who said, 'Stop
trying and start trusting.' '

> Yes. See? You first have to try, but then you simply *do,* in other
> words, stop trying, just trust. Just trust, In other words, when the
> channel is open, *it'll flow.* It'll flow. Here's an absolute. When you
> open that channel, honestly, and with unconditional love—
> whatever degree, you know, the highest degree of unconditional
> love that can be had at that time—when you open that channel,
> you will *never* be denied. It will flow. And that Christ Light will
> come through and it'll be there. It'll be there.

Although Tom didn't mention it, the Apostle Paul's encounter with the
Light of Christ on the road to Damascus has many NDE-like characteristics. In 2 Corinthians 12:2–4, he also tells of a man, clearly himself,
who "fourteen years ago was caught up to the third heaven. Whether it
was in the body or out of the body, I do not know—God knows. And I
know that this man—whether in the body or apart from the body I do
not know—but God knows—was caught up in Paradise. He heard inexpressible things, things that man is not permitted to tell."

Tom and many other NDErs say much the same thing. But what
they *are* permitted to tell, and *do,* is that God is Love, and the purpose
of life is to love God, others, and oneself unconditionally. Thus, rather
than challenging or attempting to supplant the Gospel, the NDE points
to and focuses on the central Biblical emphases of Divine love, forgiveness, and grace.

Lives
of Love

Many NDErs retain their careers after their experiences and find ways to incorporate their new values into their jobs, using much of their spare time helping others either informally or through volunteer programs. Others are drawn in new directions, many with new interests in the helping professions. One NDEr found a new calling in the hospital room where her experience took place:

> In that room were three women, all very old, all dying. I could *feel* and *sense* their tremendous fear, their terror, their loneliness and pain. I was like a sponge—I *felt* the pain, *felt* the terror. I had always been a sensitive person, but this was much more. I was overwhelmed by this and by their tremendous loneliness. I vowed at that moment that when I was better, I would do something to help people who are dying.

Elaine Winner, like many NDErs, finds her experience has given her a particularly strong empathy for, and ability to help, the terminally ill. She describes her feelings and experiences with them:

> The dying person needs to feel that even though they have this shortened space of time, the things they have to impart to the living are just as valuable as if they were going to continue to live. The aspect of being able to *receive* as well as *give* is just as great a gift.

> One lady who was dying said she needed some time, she wanted to be able to give to her kids. And I said, "Do you want to cheat them out of a valuable gift—to be able to give? Perhaps the reason you're here, in this state, is to be able to learn to receive. Because it's always been you that's given, and the kids have received. Now the tables are turned." And she thought for a little bit, and didn't say anything. And I said, "What is it, _____, are you afraid of not being able to give? Is it that you're frustrated with a body that will not do what you want it to do? Or is it a thing of your coming up and realizing that you're facing death, that death is an inevitable thing? Are you afraid of pain at death? Or are you afraid of what's beyond death?"

> She nodded in agreement [to all these questions]. And I said to her, "Didn't I ever tell you that my own heart stopped, and that I had taken one step beyond and come back? First of all, let me describe something to you. You have a life force. A tree has a life force. That soul, that life force, has lived from infinity, and it goes to infinity. It doesn't stop anywhere along the way. And just as a tree has to gain new leaves in spring, so that soul has to take on a new body in order

for the soul or spirit to grow. Just as the leaves die in the fall, so you have to shed your physical body. It just goes. For some people, it's an instantaneous death, for other people it's a more prolonged death, as in your case. However we go, there's a lesson from it to be learned, by the living. If the living will just learn.

And I told her there was no pain in death, and I went on to describe my own experience, and I let her know that when she does die, there's no pain there, that it's nothing more than blinking her eye or going from one room to another. When my heart stopped, that being of mine was still there, even though I knew I had felt something of mine behind. I wasn't at all concerned with what I had left behind. It's like taking off a favorite coat. And she said, "I never thought of that." And I also told her that at death, she wouldn't be alone, that someone who had gone before her would be there to help guide her. And I also told her, "You've given to your kids, you've done the best you know how, you've learned a lot of your lessons the hard way." All this seemed to help her a great deal.

Another NDEr, a woman in her thirties with three children and a husband, was walking by a nursing home not long after her experience and felt herself drawn to go inside. Overwhelmed with compassion for the elderly patients, she offered her services as a volunteer and soon undertook nurse's training. She now works with the terminally ill in a hospice.

One of the most consistent aftereffects of NDEs is a greatly reduced fear of death. In a study conducted by Kenneth Ring and myself (see Table 1), 18 of 21 sampled NDErs indicated they had strongly decreased fear of death, the other three indicating some decrease. Many NDErs understandably find they have great capacity to work with the dying. One who works as a volunteer in a nursing home told me "I've helped people die. My role with older people is to help them accept death. A couple of times, I've felt like an angel. I've literally taken a few people by the hand and prepared them to die, at the last minute."

Barbara Harris found a special calling due to her newfound empathy with the terminally ill. She said, "Compassion in medicine is my mission, my goal. In becoming a respiratory therapist, I wanted to work one on one, putting my hands all over sick people, helping to draw them back to health. I found that my expertise was in intensive care. Whenever I had my hands on comatose patients, I had this wonderful feeling of telepathy."

Many NDErs counsel the terminally ill and other people in need on an informal basis. One older lady who is sought out by many terminally ill and grief-stricken people who hear about her and come to her home told me:

> When I came back from the experience, I knew I had something to do. I knew when the time came I would be given whatever I needed to do it. I didn't choose this work. He [God] brought it right to my door. There are times when people call me, saying they have a problem with a person who is dying. And they'll come to me. It happens all the time.
>
> Before somebody comes, I'm always a little scared because I don't want to say the wrong thing and hurt them or set them back or something. I'm always afraid of that. You don't always know if you're doing it right. I always go into my Bible. I *depend* on God. He gives me things to help people. I don't know how this happens, but sometimes He will give me something and I will talk to somebody, and I don't remember what I said; it's as if He gives it to me.

Like the vast majority of NDErs I talked with, this lady accepts no money for her help, despite difficult economic circumstances (her husband is retired, and they both live on Social Security). In her words:

> We don't do these things because we're trying to gain anything, but because we're living out the love of God that we experienced. Whatever we do, we do *freely*, with our whole heart. Just like we accept God freely, without any reservations. It's not for a purpose but just because we love. Period. If you do it for love, that's the greatest pleasure for the person who's doing it. And *that's* your reward, if you're looking for a reward.

Two other NDErs reflected the same spirit:

> I used to help people once in a while, but I used to think, "Well, maybe he or she can help me sometime." I would say, "Well, maybe you can pay me back sometime." Now I don't expect payment. It's so opposite—as opposite as can be.
>
> The quality of love I give to others is different now. Love, to me, doesn't have to be returned anymore. Even if I get nothing from the other person, it doesn't offend me. I don't feel badly. I get such a joy of showing love and tenderness to a person in a nursing home.

Many NDErs I encountered are in fairly uncertain, though not destitute, financial situations, in large part because of generous in ways that others might regard as being taken advantage of. One NDEr described her feelings about this in a way that reflects typical NDEr attitudes:

> Before the NDE, I wouldn't let anybody take advantage of me. But now I realize that you can allow yourself to be taken advantage of, not only for the good of others but also for yourself—when you help somebody else, you benefit from it, too. Before the experience, generally I wouldn't help anybody because I was, in a sense, selfish. Looking out for number one.

NDErs whose experiences took place at formative times during their lives find the NDE impelling them in previously unthought-of directions. One whose NDE took place in her late teens stated:

> I was a typical college girl who didn't care much about my studies. Before the experience, I didn't know what I wanted to do. Afterwards, I would look at people and see their actual soul, their essence. It was almost as though it was a big light. I saw the total personality. This helped me to look at people with emotional problems and see that they are very good, loving people who are very frightened and are doing what they are doing because of that. I could empathize with them much more than before.

Sharon gave up a lucrative career to work as a volunteer:

> After the experience, I began to work with emotionally disturbed children. Beforehand, I had a tendency to shy away from people like that, but afterward, I was very comfortable working with them. I felt *absolutely* comfortable with them. Beforehand, whenever I'd try anything like that, I would quit, because I'd think, "I don't know what to do with these kids, What do I do with them? They're different." They weren't like anyone else I'd known. But after the NDE, I began to see them as separate little individuals with worth, and I'd think, "Whatever this little child can do, take it and go with it. Expand on it." Before the NDE, I had a sort of pessimistic outlook on things like that.

Barbara Harris became a respiratory therapist after her experience. In that profession, as well as in her informal counseling and relating to others, she often finds herself dealing with people who have various kinds of both physical and emotional problems. She related two instances in which her NDE-related empathy and willingness to help had a strong impact.

First, Barbara told me of a younger man who was her fellow trainee in respiratory therapy. She had driven him to work every day and noticed the poor neighborhood he lived in, and though he was very quiet, she did her utmost to help him and give him a positive attitude toward the training program and life in general. They both did very well on their final exams, and they were overjoyed when they received job offers in respiratory therapy:

> Two weeks later, he took me out to lunch with his first paycheck. He pulled up his sleeves and he showed me the scars on his wrists. And he gave me a copy of the book *Catcher in the Rye,* and he told me I had been his "catcher in the rye" and that the day before school had started, he had tried to commit suicide, and when he came to the school, it was the kind of thing where if he didn't click into this, he was going to do it again, only this time really.

NDErs are often able to "see beneath the surfaces" of people, as in the case of Barbara's response to an older man who was not what he outwardly seemed when Barbara went out of her way to help him.

> One day when I was coming to work at the hospital where I was being trained as a respiratory therapist, I saw a man in front of the hospital, which was in a slum area. Everyone had passed him by, thinking he was a derelict, as there were many in the area. But I couldn't walk past him. I couldn't get in the door; it was like this wall that was keeping me out. I took his pulse and it was racing. I tried to talk to him, and he was real disoriented. A couple of my fellow therapists saw me trying to help him, came outside, and told me that the man was just a drunk. "No," I said, "this man is going to die!" Well, one thing led to another and I got into an argument with one of my colleagues, who wouldn't let me put the man in my car to take him to the heart hospital. Finally, the ambulance came and took him away, after he had tried to run away although he was sick.
>
> After I got out of work, I found a message that he was at the Heart Institute, so I drove over there. I walked into a private room with a private nurse and his beautifully coiffed and dressed wife who threw

her arms around me and said to me, "You know, you saved my husband's life. The doctor said he would have lived maybe another half hour—he was in arrhythmia and a few other things."

We became real good friends. He was an attorney, a retired attorney, who had started a halfway house program for prisoners that came out of the Miami jail, where he would place them in homes of other retired attorneys so that they could get a chance. And he counseled them himself. He was a *beautiful* man. He was very wealthy, but he went out walking every morning near the hospital where I worked, and he dressed very casually every morning when he went out walking.

Somehow, when all this happened, it was as though I had no choice. I *had* to stay with this man and help him, because I *knew* he would have died if I didn't. Later, after he recovered but found out he was terminally ill, I acted as his confidant. I helped him work out a lot of things, like his feeling estranged from his wife and daughter. I helped him resolve these things, and he died about two years after our first encounter.

After he died, his wife wrote and told me that after he talked to me, they had a most romantic twenty-fifth wedding anniversary and that he had reconciled with his daughter. I mean, he did all these really neat things, and then he died. So it gave him an extra two years, because none of this business had been finished. And in those two years that he lived, he just did everything that he was supposed to do. I went to that memorial service and I just sobbed, because whoever wanted to just got up and talked about him. And that was just an incredible time for me, because I really felt like I had helped this man.

One of the most moving experiences I had doing the research for this book occurred when I visited the home of another NDEr who, after her experience, began to take disabled children into her home from state institutions. I will never forget the look of peace and contentment on the face of a little blind girl whose real parents had abandoned her and who had since, along with several other children, received this woman's devoted love.

Another NDEr was profoundly moved not long after her experience when she saw several young children walking into a juvenile detention facility. She inquired about them and found they were poor children who had been arrested for stealing food but had been put together with older, more hardened delinquents. Overwhelmed with compassion, she immediately began investigating ways the juvenile justice system might be changed to protect the younger offenders. This led to her development of an innovative program, which gained such attention that she was invited to part of the White House Conference on Juvenile Delinquency. Before her experience she had been, in her words, "a mousy, withdrawn housewife," who had never engaged in any public activities.

Such compassion also strongly influences the many NDErs who return to the jobs they had before their experience. One man in his forties, a school administrator, stated:

> Though I was always dedicated to the betterment of students before the NDE, I had always been more of a "corporate man." You know, if the boss said, "This is the way it's going to be," I'd say, "Okay." Now, I don't have a fear that if I go against a superior and am threatened with my job, I'll lose my house and my family will starve. Now, what I believe in, and what I believe is in the best interests of the students, is most important, and I won't compromise that at *any* cost.

At the time I interviewed him, this man was putting his beliefs into practice in a situation in which he was risking his career in support of retaining a program that had substantially benefited many working-class students, in opposition to his boss, who wanted the program canceled.

It is important to remember, however, that the vast majority of NDErs' loving actions take place informally, in a multitude of contexts and interactions. But on the job or through spontaneous encounters, NDErs often affect others profoundly. One said:

> I don't see myself as an NDEr who is affecting others' lives. I see myself as a person who has had a near-death experience, and, as a result, there are some capacities that I have that might help other people. To me, it's as if something comes *through* me, and that it's not me. It's like I'm handy, I'm just like a tool. I'm a facilitator for . . . like one of the Blues Brothers, I'm on a mission from God. Listen, that television program "Highway to Heaven" gets to me, for that reason. Exactly.

TIMMY SAWYER

It would be impossible to chronicle fully in any representative manner all the countless ways NDErs affect others' lives. One interesting possibility is that NDErs will "pass on" to their children traits of compassion, empathy, and caring. While no extensive study has been done of this, I came across a most interesting and heartening instance of this while visiting Tom Sawyer and his family. Tom has two sons. Todd, now in his mid-teens, was about ten when his father's NDE took place, and he was not influenced by the "new" Tom as much as his younger brother Timmy, who was about two when it took place.

Todd is, as his father was before the NDE, an "all-American boy." He is an expert mechanic, and his room is filled with pictures of cars, trucks, and his pretty girlfriend. A most responsible youth, Todd nonetheless does not exhibit much of the strong spirituality his father came to exhibit after his experience.

Timmy, however, does. Since he was around six years old, he has demonstrated an amazingly precocious capacity to help people, particularly elderly residents of nursing homes. Timmy has helped so many patients in various nursing homes and is so effective at it that the staff in these facilities have given him virtually complete access to the patients, and some have even placed him "on call" in that many patients will request that he come and talk to and be with them. All other ten-year-old boys are barred; indeed, no child younger than sixteen is allowed in, even to visit relatives!

> Timmy has an *extraordinary* capacity for philosophy; he's a miniature philosopher. And wisdom. That's rare. But on an ongoing basis, he automatically derives his pleasure from helping others. I mean, if he can go without, and have four or five people be extraordinarily happy, he will derive as much pleasure as the four people who will have the candy, or whatever. Tim will typically always be concerned with how what he does might make others more comfortable.

> Timmy has carte blanche in this huge nursing home, the whole building, where there are about a thousand patients. He can go from floor to floor. Now, legally, an adult visitor, even if some relative of ours is there, does not have permission to go to another

floor and push somebody in a wheelchair. Timmy knows everybody in the building, and they have allowed him, since he was eight years old, to push people in the wheelchairs, go in any of the rooms, and they call, on the telephone, and request that we sent Tim to spend time at the home.

It's incredible the effect he has on the patients. Some of the patients there are in decrepit shape, and he is able to talk to them and communicate with them on a deep level.

Timmy's exceptional spiritual gifts extend to other kinds of people as well. Tom and his wife Elaine told me of several retarded children he has related to and helped:

Without talking about it, Timmy has the ability to see the unconditional love in another person, such as a child with Down's syndrome. You know how often a ten-year old child will ridicule or complain about such a person? But if you want to see something extraordinary, come by sometime and see how kindly and lovingly he relates to such kids.

NANCY CLARK

In the strict sense, Nancy Clark is not an NDEr. Her experience occurred when she was giving a eulogy for a friend. When she started giving the eulogy, she saw the Light and was given a message to promulgate love and foster harmony throughout the world.

After her experience, Nancy showed the same pattern of life changes that we have seen to be characteristic of NDErs' transformations. She exudes a deep spirituality that deeply moves all who come in contact with her, and like NDErs, she has helped many people. Like NDErs, she feels herself used as an instrument of God's love and is often able to convey this love to others who previously had not been affected by clergy or other religious or spiritual avenues from which they had sought help.

Nancy explains the mandate of love that has been her sole motivation since her experience:

The Light—God—has given me a calling, the profound work to do for Him, and that is simply to teach others about love, His love and human love, and to promulgate his message to the masses of people.

In a very strong sense, I simply need to channel those feelings to other people, rather than to verbalize or intellectualize about it in any way. I don't feel I possess the intellectual awareness of who God is, what God is, or what His intentions and purposes are. Rather, God has truly infused Himself into me and reveals Himself to me as this inexpressible LOVE residing deep within me. It was not a love that transformed me only for those few moments of my experience, just sweeping into me and just floating out of me, but rather this incredibly unhuman love was infused into every cell of my physical human body. It is this love, that is not human, that I carry with me. It is this love that needs to find an outlet that can be channeled to other human beings, not because of my desire. It [the love] is God, and we are all a part of God. We were created as a spark from Him, this divine energy, this divine love, and so we are, at some level of awareness, some level of existence, a part of Him. Whether we want to accept it or not, we are . . . we must simply yield and let go and allow His energy to flow through us, and thereby emerge as the total human beings we were created to be.

I think many people don't yield to it; they're not made aware of it. They may know about this intellectually, but they haven't begun to spiritually accept it.

This energy I feel inside of me, this profound love, is my gift. It is a calling I was meant to use. Again, I am only a channel, through which this love can manifest itself to human beings.

The love that God infused in me is not content to remain locked within me, to be kept for my own personal use and needs. So powerful is this force that I feel compelled to give it to others, not so much for my own human need to give it away but rather from the divine presence working through me, speaking out and seeking more opportunties to manifest more of His presence to others through me. This pure unconditional love is a beautiful gift that is being offered to others through me, and all one has to do is to accept it.

One morning I received an unexpected phone call from a man on the staff of the university where I teach. He told me he had seen a videotape of a recent conference on NDEs that the university had sponsored and at which Nancy had spoken.

Though the other NDErs had also affected him, Nancy's talk had transformed his life. He described the impact she had on him, which has continued and grown even though he has met her only once, in a letter he sent to her not long after he had seen her talk:

> I really don't know how to begin this letter to you, so I will begin. I want to thank you for "being there" and being able to hear you at the workshop held at the university in April. I wasn't there at the time, but I did see the videotape of the conference on a station in Cincinnati where I live. I must tell you that I was *moved* by your experience.
>
> The effect on me has been nothing short of miraculous and I have since contacted Dr. Charles Flynn to find out where I could write to you. I merely wanted to explain the effect your talk had on me and the positive changes in my life that have occurred since. I attribute these changes to the "spirituality" that emanated from your testimony.
>
> For the last six months I've been involved in Al-Anon and O.A. (Overeaters Anonymous), both 12-step self-help groups affiliated with A.A. I live with a recovering alcoholic and I suffer from the emotional ramifications of this disease. Through Al-Anon and O.A. I am learning how to live with myself and review my own sense of self-worth.
>
> An integral part—if not the most significant part—of the programs is the belief in a "power greater than ourselves who could restore us to health." Whether we choose to call this power God is not important. What is important is that this loving presence must be actualized before any significant recovery can begin. This is true no matter what chemical is used as the addictive substance—alcohol, drugs, food, tobacco. This concept is the "spirituality" of the program.
>
> On a Sunday night, June 3, I found myself watching a video of Dr. Flynn's workshop on TV. Originally, I wasn't going to watch it, but something inside of me compelled me to see it. When you began to talk I became overwhelmed by a peaceful sense that is hard for me to describe. For some reason, I "knew" what you were saying was true, authentic, genuine, and both "thrills and chills" went through me. I was captivated by this wonderful sense of tranquillity and reassurance when you spoke of "unconditional love." I "knew" what you meant, and I could feel the genuine sense of happiness

you felt when you said, "This experience—this love—is going to happen to *all* of you!"

The result for me has been dramatic. For the last twenty-one years I've attempted to stop smoking. Nicotine—cigarettes—tobacco has been my compulsive addiction. I *couldn't* stop—and the many times I tried left me with awful guilt and low self-esteem. It was not a matter of my "will power" over a cigarette. I suppose my problem was that I really didn't believe that a power greater than myself could—and would—help me overcome this addiction. I still doubted. My God was an overwhelming, awesome mega-power that I saw in the Catholic church. If I begged long enough to this God, He *might* help me. It was a supplicating relationship and one not based on mutual love, God was the all-knowing parent. I was the supplicating, errant child. I was only told that love existed between us, and I could only believe that there "might be."

As I heard your testimony, I became filled with a presence. I knew then there was such a spirit—there was such a deep and abiding relationship and there *is* a wonderful bond between we humans and the Creator. I knew I could submit myself to the will of this loving spirit because I am here on this earth to seek Him out. I knew then that God was not deceitful, that I was not made to suffer, and I wasn't here as some cosmic joke. As they say in A.A., "God doesn't make garbage." I know from the sublimeness of your talk that there is a pure and spiritual love that no one can ever understand until that time we are to embrace it as it happened with you. It is important for me to know that love exists—it *is*—it unquestionably *is*. That was significant to me. I prayed later that I could conquer my unhealthly addiction.

The next day, in the morning, just after I arrived at work, I was hit with a terrific urge to smoke. I asked God to help me. At that moment the urge broke and a rush of relief swept all through my body. I knew then I could *do it*—I could make it through withdrawal. I didn't fear it, and no anxiety was too great to overcome. Suddenly the "spirituality" I heard talked about in the A.A. programs became a reality and it became clear why this reliance and understanding of a Higher Power is so necessary. I've never been a religious person, but now I pray, and I pray only that God's will be done in my life one day at a time, and that I can live according to that plan.

I believe I was meant to see your testimony and experience this wonderful reaffirmation. I want to thank you and let you know your healing spirit can radiate from a videotape through a TV set.

Thank you again and I hope your healing continues and the spirit within you radiates out to more people who need it.

Nancy has also helped many others, particularly those in need of spiritual strength, such as suicide attempters. In Nancy's words:

> I've worked with people who are suicidal, who felt so unloved that life had no meaning for them. One person told me she didn't know how to love and didn't want to risk being hurt. Evidently this was a way of life for her—people she loved would always desert her. Her pain was so great she considered suicide. She had seen psychiatrists, but they were not able to be helpful to her.
>
> I came into contact with her through someone who had heard me speak at a conference. She telephoned me, and I began to work with her, and before long she began taking risks, becoming the recipient of a "love that passeth all understanding." Today she is radiant and giving more of herself to others and feeling good about herself.
>
> Now, I'm not a psychiatrist, and I'm not familiar with professional counseling methods. I wouldn't presume to know how to help anyone on my own. But, again, once I enter into that beautiful state of pure love, then what comes forth are not my own therapeutic insights but rather the insights that spring forth from some other source, this source coming from the Light, or the divine spirit, within me who knows the needs of a person I am working with. It is His love that provides the gift of healing for that person. He simply allows me, I guess is the best word, to have that insight into that particular person's needs so that I am able to—so that *He* is able to—use my human voice to get those words out so that individual will be able to hear and accept the gift that is being offered.
>
> Afterwards, when I reflect upon the situation, I will often say, "How did I know to say that?" Or I'll become awed at the fact that somehow I knew exactly what to say to meet that person's specific need. But, you see, *I* didn't know what to say, but the spirit of pure love did, and brought it forth so lovingly.
>
> These are some of my most precious moments, when I acknowledge the true source within me, bringing forth this love and healing to others through me.
>
> After my counseling sessions, so to speak, in the privacy of prayer, I channel all my human love—and more—to the Light in thanksgiving for the beautiful way He channels His love to others through

me. As I do this, I become bathed in the richness of His pure love, and every cell in my body is saturated with this beautiful love. It is so overwhelming an experience to have my emotions burst forth in an outpouring of tears and joy, intermingled. Afterwards, I'm so refreshed and revitalized and strengthened to travel along the path of life that the Light—God—has called me to travel on, for *His* glory, not mine.

It is this deep, abiding love that resides within me that provides everything I need to sustain me through life. Love is the true sustenance of the soul. It's seeing something in another person that they themselves cannot see, perhaps because they have blinders on or because of their own fears or insecurity.

Because of my experience, I can look at others the way the Light sees them. I don't push them, just try to help them, giving them a little bit of my strength for that moment that they are fearful or insecure. And sometimes that's all it takes, just giving your strength a little to someone.

Love is showing appreciation for another person, and taking that responsibility to show or direct that appreciation to that individual. Let them know! Let them know that you like what they have contributed, whether it was something large or something very, very small. Let people know.

Nancy's new calling began not long after her experience. The son of the man who had died in the plane accident and for whom she was giving the eulogy when her experience occurred had for a long time been depressed and suicidal. His father's death made him even more negative about life.

Since this young man had known Nancy before the experience, his comments about how she was transformed are, like Ron's comments about A.J., very helpful in understanding the kind of impact NDErs have on nonexperiencers:

Before she had her experience with the Light, Nancy was more reserved and more complacent. After her experience with the Light, her personality showed more confidence and sureness and boldness and control—much more control, it seems. Before her experience, it seemed that fear had a greater hold on her. Afterwards, the presence of fear seemed to have disappeared completely.

Before her experience, I was not aware of her deeper concern or her feelings that she had for other human beings. When I came to see her after her experience, there was a great and beautiful trust that came to me, which just took hold of and relieved my fears and anxieties. Because of that trust, her life has been a great blessing to me. I can relate to her my deeper feelings and deeper emotions and deeper spiritual subjects that I really have need of expressing to another human being. And I found that she was the only one I could express these deeper spiritual matters to, with the confidence that I would not be judged negatively for any of my feelings or my emotions. That relationship has been very precious to me. It's the greatest gift I think I've received from her.

Nancy has definitely given greater meaning to my life. I have a deeper desire to love others, not for something they have done for me or what kindness or things I have received from them. She has given unconditionally because of who they are—because they are a child of God even though they have characteristics or things that would make me feel unpleasantly toward them or make me not want to love them. She has shown me how to love them, in a deeper way, in a way that God would love and the way that God has loved me.

She's given me more meaning in life, so as to look at something not in a negative way, but to look at everything as positive. This has given me a better understanding of death, especially my father's death, because I can look at my father's death as a "positive." In my unexplainable, uncontrollable emotions and feelings, which I had no way of grasping or understanding, I reached out to God for understanding, which has brought me to a better relationship with God, and Nancy's interpretation of life has deeply helped me.

One part of my life was deeply changed [by Nancy]. I was looking at things like good and evil and dealing with the evil in a much too focused way. By spiritual understanding, she explained to me that I am free from fear of the evil one, or the negative, because the Light or the positive will protect me. But when I give it thought, or when I recognize the evil, then it becomes a reality to me. Nancy showed me that I have no need to fear any evil anymore, and that has given my life a more relaxed and calm meaning, a more genuine and positive meaning in life, with the absence of the fear of the negative.

In helping me cope with my father's death and my father's spirituality, she helped me and comforted me by giving my father as an example of this full life and this genuine Christianity, in God. When Nancy spoke to me about the experience she had with the Light, at my father's funeral, she spoke of the great love that was in the Light, and that my father's presence was with her. She told me of other people's accounts of my father's great love for God and great love for the Scriptures. This was a very emotionally uplifting experience to me and a very enlightening experience to me, not only of the love of God in His acceptance for us but of my father's existence after death. Everything she spoke of about the experience touched my "inner man," so to speak, and this gave me a wonderful joy and a beautiful peace and a beautiful acknowledgment of life after death and a comforting feeling that death is just the beginning of a new life.

Her experience has given me a better outlook on death. I look at death now as very positive. I look with anxiousness and hope that I'll experience this Light, and this same love that Nancy described, and that my father will be waiting there for me and other loved ones. My whole outlook on death has changed. I can see how death can be a healing, how my father's death may have been an ultimate healing.

Most NDErs work with others on a one-to-one basis. Could the NDE provide a seedbed for transformation on a wider level? Barbara Harris suggests that the lessons about life and death conveyed through the NDE could be the foundation of an educational experience focusing on life's greatest and most important task—learning to love others. In her words:

I can picture the world as being a pattern of relationships. And the more loving we are, the more this reality will evolve into what we all want. If we can't make these relationships loving, if we can't get to "critical mass," then the planet's just not going to make it. I've heard a lot of prophetic visions, and some of them are very dark. But I also understand alternative realities. And we have our choice here. If I can touch enough people and explain to them what I'm about, and if they can touch enough people and explain to them what they're about, and it can just keep webbing out, we've got a reality that's going to last.

If I am with a person on a one-to-one level, we together can transcend, with people that are ready, the concept of love that the planet has had up until now, and get into the feeling of unity and love and what I'm all about. And after, they're changed. They've gone through their own little transformation.

I can't begin to fathom how I could explain to you how different I am from that girl before the NDE. She was a community worker, proper mother, proper wife—but so empty, so shallow. And since that time, I'm living. I wasn't living before; I was existing. And I feel as though every experience has a joy, a meaning. My reality now is magnificent. All these things that I am now are just my being, my instrument, to help the rest of the planet evolve. That's my main concern.

I heard someone say that the whole earth is a big school, you know, like K through 12. And some of us are up to the eleventh grade, let's say, and our job is to take the kindergarten kids and the first graders and right on up, take them by the hand and help them pass to the higher grades.

10

The
Love
Project

How can the educational process foster unconditional love among those who haven't had NDEs or been directly influenced by NDErs or those who, like Nancy Clark, have been transformed by similar experiences? How can educators and others nurture greater compassion and caring within the competitive, formalized, ritualized educational context, which so often seems to inculcate negative imagery rather than transcend it?

As a professor, I had long been dissatisfied with modes of education that failed to address the most significant questions of human existence. While recognizing and applauding the substantial value of the rigorously obtained knowledge of social behavior and institutions that constitutes the body of findings in my own and related disciplines, I felt that the most central ingredient—the love that binds people together and makes any society possible and makes human life meaningful—was never directly dealt with. Moreover, was I teaching my students anything of lasting value? Though they gained understanding and insight into social and cultural patterns, institutions, and ideologies, did they really change as people in ways that would have a truly positive and lasting impact on their lives?

In pondering ways to deal with this problem, I read Leo Buscaglia's book *Love*. I had first heard him lecture on public television, and I found his critical views on dehumanizing social values and educational patterns and his beliefs of the supreme importance of love, and that love can be learned and is something behavioral rather than a mere feeling or passing emotion, a very congruent and eloquent expression of my own personal and professional views.

Love contains much trenchant social criticism, some of which stems directly from social scientists such as Pitirim Sorokin, whose *Ways and Power of Love* strongly influenced Buscaglia. I was excited also by the strong parallels with and the applicability of his insights to the subject matter of both Introductory Sociology and Social Theory, as well as other courses I taught. For example, Buscaglia has much to say about the way social stereotypes and labels, as well as social class distinctions, keep us from loving others. He also spends much time analyzing cultural values and norms that inhibit and repress loving attitudes and behavior. But most significantly, he goes beyond such analysis of what is wrong to, in his words, inspire people to begin to "live the answers." Long dissatisfied with the relatively negative diagnoses of social analysis that provide little or no guidance on how to make things better, I found that Buscaglia's ideas as well as his ebullient lecture style provided the basis for a more positive approach to social life and social problems. In very basic ways, there were strong parallels, as well, between the life-and-love affirmations of the NDE and the ways it transformed people into more loving, empathic, caring individuals and Buscaglia's belief that such values, attitudes, and behavior can be learned and promulgated.

The Love Project was a required part of the course work. In addition to reading *Love* early in the semester, students were shown videotapes of interviews with NDErs, as well as videotapes of Buscaglia's lectures on how to apply unconditional love in their lives. They were asked to relate in a loving manner to a particular individual that they would not otherwise have gotten to know—this was termed the "Love Project"—and to keep an account of their feelings and experiences in a "Love Journal," in which they were also asked to record how various aspects of the sociology course material might have helped them overcome prejudice, stereotyping, and other kinds of unloving attitudes and behavior patterns. Finally, they were asked to form small (about five or six students) "Love Groups" in which they would relate to one another in a loving way and discuss among themselves their experiences with the Love Project and the thoughts and feelings engendered by attempting to apply the *Love* book and related ideas to their lives.

The instructions read, in part:

Professor Flynn's study of the Near-Death Experience has shown that people who have this experience become much more loving, kindly, and compassionate toward others as a result of the experience. This seems to be because they believe that they encountered a God of total love and acceptance, which they refer to as the Being of Light, and they bring this love back with them and apply it in their lives. . . . The question arises, is there some way that people can try to become this way without having a Near-Death Experience? What is needed more than anything else in this world threatened by nuclear holocaust, hatred, and violence of all sorts is more love, more compassion, more kindness. If sociology and social science have any ultimate value, meaning, or purpose, they should help contribute to this. Your Love Project is a pioneering effort to find out.

A number of possible difficulties occurred to students. First, many wondered whether they should tell the person they were relating to about the project. Relating to someone simply because it is required, as one put it, might be a type of "betrayal." Moreover the very term *project* seems to depersonalize human interaction by creating, in Buber's terms, "I-It" relationships.

As the projects progressed, however, this proved not to be a problem. The project simply provided an incentive, a context, for what many students soon came to experience as genuine relationships. In those cases where students informed their project people about the assignment, the relationships had become so real and sincere that the way they happened to have begun was no longer of any substantial relevance.

A second problem emerged with students' efforts to find suitable people. Some chose to work through established volunteer programs such as Big Brother and Big Sister projects, Adopt-a-Grandparent, sorority and fraternity visits to nursing homes and tutoring programs. I found it very helpful, and indeed necessary, to inform the directors of such programs of the Love Project so they would be prepared to help students find people to relate to.

On a less formal basis, ministers were important sources of project people. I told as many ministers as I knew about the project and asked them to help students find suitable people to relate to. Religious organizations such as the United Campus Ministry were also significant sources of referrals.

As much as possible, I encouraged students to use the project as a means to relate to people associated with the kinds of careers they were planning or exploring. Many, as will be shown, found they had a strong interest in working with the elderly and to prepare for careers in the rapidly growing field of gerontology, which will need many more people in the future owing to the very large and growing proportion of the population over sixty-five. In this and other ways, the project aimed at meeting students' practical needs related to career exploration and preparation. With robotic technology and other changes rapidly transforming the work world, many future jobs will involve service activities such as helping the elderly and the handicapped, which require love and compassion and which were previously done largely on a volunteer basis. The project was thus not only an idealistic but an eminently practical and realistic learning experience.

Students also had the option of relating to someone in an informal way. Many chose roommates they had trouble getting along with, ostracized students, and family members. Some found maids and janitors in their dorms and fraternity and sorority houses, co-workers on summer and vacation jobs, and other suitable people to relate to.

In each instance, I tried to discuss students' choices and give them some guidance. Though it was difficult to do this in the large (150 to 250 students) Introductory Sociology classes as compared with the smaller advanced classes in Social Problems and Social Theory I also assigned the project to, I attempted to encourage students to develop projects that would be meaningful to their growth and development, both personally and, for the more advanced students, in terms of career experience and preparation. The "Love Groups" provided a basis for students with similar projects to "compare notes" and encourage one another as well as share insights and understanding they were obtaining from their experiences during the last parts of class sessions.

In addition, I showed several tapes of Leo Buscaglia's speeches at various times throughout the semester. This proved not only highly popular but very motivating to students.

Students were somewhat puzzled at first by the unfamiliar and relatively unstructured nature of the Love Project and related assignments. Since it goes against the trend of the prevalent ethic of "looking out for number one" and involves time and commitment, some students cynically dismissed it. However, many found it an extraordinarily valuable experience. It was not very long before my teaching assistant Marilyn Adams, who played a central role in the inception of the project, and I began to be encouraged by students' reports they were gaining a great deal from the projects and journals. But it wasn't until the class was nearly over that the full extent of the effectiveness of the new approach became apparent.

At the conclusion of the course, I collected the Love Journals and accounts of the Love Projects and administered a questionnaire, which contained some of the same items that were administered by Ring and myself (see Table 1), with a number of additional items pertaining to personal growth and values more pertinent to the course material and purposes. In addition, I also used the Love Project, in slightly modified form, as an assignment in several advanced Sociology courses, including Social Problems, Social Theory, and Social Conflict. Table 3 presents the combined results of the questionnaires I administered to all of my students, a total of 428; all answered anonymously.

The results show that the Love Project has a substantial capacity to provide a basis for growth in concern for others, personal growth of various kinds, and a somewhat lesser degree of value change. Although the courses and the Love Projects had no specifically religious content, I also asked participants if any of their religious orientations had changed in order to compare this with patterns among NDErs. A minority showed some change in religious attitudes, as well as, interestingly enough, change in attitudes toward death and the afterlife.

In the "concern for others" category, for example, about twenty percent indicated strong increases in the desire to help others, compassion for others, acceptance of others, and insight into others' problems, with about approximately another two-thirds indicating some increases and a small minority no change. Virtually none indicated decreased concern for others. Though less striking, the Love Project participants indicated strong (eleven percent) and some (fifty-four percent) increases in self-worth and self-esteem, and well over half indicated either strong or some increases in their sense of meaning and purpose in life, positive relationships with their families, and self-understanding (nineteen percent strong, fifty-eight percent some increase).

With the exception of a presentation and discussion during one class period of the NDE in each class, accompanied by a brief lecture on its relevance to sociological concerns, the Love Project participants did not focus on the NDE or on death-related issues. Nonetheless, the Love Project led to some (twenty-two percent) and strong (four percent) decreases in fear of death among the students, and nearly one-third overall (five percent strong, twenty-five percent some) indicated increases in their belief in an afterlife. Likewise, though the substantial majority indicated no changes in their religious perspectives, one fourth (two percent strong, twenty-three percent some) indicated increased sense of God's inner presence and nearly the same number (four percent strong, eighteen percent some) increases in their belief in a higher power. This is understandable, since the purpose of the Love Project was not specifically religious in the sense of particular belief systems and I made a conscious effort to avoid couching the Project in terms of religious orientations.

Much of the success of the Project must be accorded to Buscaglia's book *Love,* which many students "took to heart," as it were. The Project, in effect, gave them the opportunity to put into practice his ideas and precepts. If such results can be attained through the use of the *Love* book and Love Project as merely part of various courses, even greater results could reasonably be expected if the Project were the central element of a specific course focused exclusively on love.

Regardless of their eventual application to society as a whole, there is little doubt that the projects have a substantial capacity for helping students learn to become more loving and compassionate. This potential was most apparent in the many Love Journal accounts chronicling dramatic, often touching, and sometimes extremely moving experiences of students overcoming various kinds of barriers to relating lovingly to others. One woman student who visited children in a nearby children's home, for example, stated:

> These kids—this project—gave me a whole new perspective. The kids are from all backgrounds, and for the first time in my life, I accepted the kids as kids, with no preconceived notions of what they'd be like. And for every time I did something or said something nice, I got a warm response. For every bit of friendship I gave to them, the kids gave it back a thousandfold. I can't think of specific incidents—we spent so much time just playing ball and talking to the kids. It's just the feelings that grew from giving. And it was wonderful.

Many others made similar comments:

> I have noticed a real change in my attitude since taking this class. I've become more considerate towards other people's feelings. I put myself in their shoes before saying something that might offend them.

> I think I have really learned a lot through this love project. The biggest thing that I've learned is that there are people in this world, and even in our home towns just dying for love, and someone to give it to them. Just because this project is over doesn't mean that I'm going to stop reaching out to Teddy [the underprivileged child he related to in his Love Project] and other kids like him.

Several students with experiences similar to these have become motivated to gain more knowledge about such growing fields as gerontology and even to investigate career possibilities in fields related to their projects. But most cited a growth in their capacities to love and relate to others whom they had previously shunned, such as students ostracized as "weirdos" and others they would normally have avoided. One student chose as her Love Project a girl living on her corridor who seemed shy, unfriendly, and reclusive and was avoided and labeled a "weirdo" by her corridor mates. During the semester, my student came to know the girl and was deeply affected by the experience:

> In getting to know her I discovered she wasn't always depressed. She's just normally solemn or unexcited. I always enjoy putting a smile on her face. Becoming familiar with her helped me to grow because I saw how beneficial it can be to put all prejudices and stereotypes aside and allow myself to love someone who may be an "individual" rather than a follower. We both benefited—I gained personal satisfaction and she gained a friend who cares.
>
> It is pretty obvious that I've gained a lot from this class. I can feel how I've grown to be a more loving person and feel how much it satisfies me to be this way. It is easier for me to relate to others now, which is something I desperately needed to improve in. If what I have to learn is as beneficial as what I already have learned, then I'll be a very fortunate, very loving, very happy person.

This is all the more remarkable, as she had to overcome considerable internal obstacles:

> To be totally honest, the first day of class I wanted to drop out. The special topic—love—scared me, and I wasn't sure why. I think it was the thought of opening up to someone I didn't know and being expected to love them. It was hard enough to express my feelings to my closest friends, let alone a stranger. But as the class progressed I slowly felt the emotional barriers break away.

Quite a number of Love Projects were work-related. One student told of a loving relationship he developed with an elderly black co-worker in a lumberyard on a job he had during summer and spring break. Another wrote a lengthy, moving account about a relationship of love that developed between herself and another young woman from the lower socioeconomic class with whom she was working as a waitress and whom she had formerly snubbed. A woman student who works part time in a department store used as her Love Project customers who "hassled" her and had previously caused her substantial irritation and distress:

> It was always hard for me to keep my cool and play the role of salesperson when customers gripe about things I have no control over. Well, this weekend a woman was giving me a hard time over our

check approval process. Although I usually get mad inside, I never say anything. This time, though, I didn't even get angry inside. I was able to step out of my role as a salesperson into her role as a customer. After she left, I smiled to myself, so proud that I had actually mastered one facet of a loving person—the ability to place myself in someone else's shoes.

Another student commented:

> I feel like reaching out to people, not only to strangers but to people I know who I don't necessarily like. I recently went back to work, and I found out that I feel differently about people who I worked with last year. I used to hate this one girl and now I don't. I said "Hi!" to her the first day back and she was surprised. Also, there is one guy at work I didn't like much. But now I realize I wasn't really giving him a chance. I treated him like he was an idiot. I began to wonder what would happen if I listened to him thoughtfully when he talked and if I talked to him seriously. This is going to be my ongoing project for this summer. Last summer I was not nice to people at work, but this summer I am going to be different.

A popular Love Project context involved students trying to relate in more loving ways to roommates who had irritated them. One girl wrote a lengthy account of her successful efforts to build a more positive relationship with a roommate whose personal habits had led to great antagonism between them. She summarizes the gradual transformation throughout the semester:

> My frustrations with my roommate just kept building and building. I found myself in continual bad moods because I kept dwelling on the negative. I was always depressed and would get mad at the drop of a hat. Finally, I started the Love Project and decided to face the problem, not turn my back to it. I started to observe her from a distance and to try and understand the motives for her actions. I tried to put myself in her shoes. I came to the conclusion that she was just ignorant of any other life style and that spite was not one of her motives.
>
> I now try to listen to her and understand her problems. I now have a more loving attitude instead of hate. I try not to let her get to me, and I honestly try to help. Before, when my attitudes were closed, neither of us was gaining; now we both gain. I have learned pa-

tience and understanding, and I think she has learned to calm down.

It has really helped to dig down deep inside myself in order to live in a more loving way. It helps to settle problems that would otherwise seem impossible.

PERSONAL AND
SOCIAL GROWTH

Love Projects often involved ostracized students. Many helped fellow students who had been looked down upon by others. One woman had noticed a young man who seemed arrogant and aloof, and she decided he would be the person she would relate to. She described her changing perceptions of him:

> For my Love Project I chose an individual with whom I had been acquainted for some time but hadn't really gotten to know very well. We met last year, and my initial impression of him was that he was the absolute antithesis of myself. He *was* very preppy, and he struck me as being arrogant. . . . I felt he was a spoiled rich kid who was very judgmental toward others. He seemed to want to remain an island—always burying himself in his studies . . . He struck me as insensitive and cold. He has a very sarcastic wit, and when I first met him I took his comments that were directed at me very personally, making me feel like he thought I was a bad person and should just shrivel up and die. However, even though I felt all these things about him, I still felt there was much more to him than he was letting anyone see.

> When we were assigned the Love Project, and after I read *Love*, I felt that I had the needed incentive to get to know this person better. The Love Project was a way for me to do something that I really wanted to do but was just too scared to go ahead and do it.

> I decided that the best way to approach this would be when we were all out with friends or something. I would build up to the point where I could ask him to do something—just the two of us, like go for a walk or study. It worked out that I didn't have to do the asking because he started asking me to do things. The more time we started spending together the easier it was for me to apply the ideas of the book *Love*. We would go for long walks and he would talk and talk and I would listen, and many times I was surprised at the

things he had to say. The arrogant prep was really a very deep, caring, sensitive individual. I found out he wasn't really arrogant, he was just kind of shy and somewhat scared of people (especially girls), and as a result of the way he dressed, people perceived him as arrogant. I tried (I am still trying) to help him realize that there is no reason to be scared of people—we're all human beings, and in the ultimate analysis we all just want to be loved and accepted. I've tried to get him to realize how much he has going for him and what a great person he is and how much he has to offer others. I've made some great progress—it's funny (but great) to hear him talk now and reiterate some of the things I've told him. I think he just needed someone to point those things out to him. I've also tried to get him to understand that he should be more accepting of others because we are all humans. He used to get disgusted at stupid things that people do, but I've tried to get him to realize that you have to put yourself in that individual's position and you have to remember that everyone has something good to offer. I've gotten him to open up and realize that sharing your feelings with others is what makes life great—he doesn't need to be such a rock or island. I think he is realizing that material success is not really as important as meaningful relationships with other people.

I do think I have helped this person a lot through the Love Project, but I can only hope I've helped him half as much as he has helped me. I have gained the greatest friend through this experience. He is very supportive of me, and he won't let me get by just doing my second best. I have learned so much from him. We don't have a lot in common, but we keep open minds. We come from totally separate worlds, but it makes our friendship better because we are exposed to each other's viewpoints and can gain another perspective.

I think we have both gained a lot through this friendship, and that helps to give us confidence. I mean I think he feels that he can tell me anything and I'll listen and still be his friend, and I think he needed to know that someone could care that much. I've seen it help a lot in his relating to others.

This experience has really meant a lot to me—it is one of the most positive of my college career. It taught me a lot about myself—that I really can reach out to someone I don't particularly see eye-to-eye with and gain a great friend as a result.

Many others found their social skills and capacity to develop friendships and relationships substantially enhanced. These were year-later follow-up comments:

After going through this project, I feel I can talk with anyone and start a relationship with them, even people who I couldn't stand before. This has really changed my disposition on life. I know that from now on, I will treat everyone in the way that I would like to be treated. I now make a conscientious effort to listen and understand when people talk to me. Even though I felt uncomfortable at first, the benefits I received out of my Love Project far outweigh the uneasy feelings. It really helped me to grow as a person and understand the problems and similarities that can occur between two seemingly different people.

I tend to try to appreciate others' problems more and to be more tolerant of them. And I am not nearly as judgmental as I used to be.

The Love Project opened my mind to a new way of looking at people and loving them. You have to open up to other people if you want them to open up to you. I have since related to many more people than I did before I took the class. I feel the Love Project is one of the greatest, most needed courses to be taught on a college campus. It is especially good at this time in a young person's life, since now is the time when you have to learn to live with *many* people all at once, and once you get out of college, you can use this information throughout your life and never feel like you're out in the world alone.

Because of the Love Project I have learned to look at people in a different way. I am quick to look for the good in people rather than automatically assuming there is something bad. I am much more tolerant of people different than myself—as a matter of fact, I am genuinely interested in their differences.

What kinds of effects does the project have on those my students relate to? For the most part, students reported that the people they related to seemed to benefit substantially from the project. As I was completing this book, I received a Christmas card from a student who had taken an advanced sociology course when I first assigned the Love Project and had related to a Mexican American teenage delinquent who, at the time, was having great difficulty in school and seemed headed for a life of crime. She wrote:

Do you remember my "Love Project"—Chico? Well, he will be

graduating from high school in June! He also was the most valuable player on his high school football team. I went to most of his games and felt like a proud parent. He has come such a long way!

That the Love Project has a strong positive effect on those the students relate to is apparent from a letter sent to one of my students from a previously somewhat shy, reclusive girl whom she befriended through the project. Both were gracious enough to allow me to share it with you:

> Of all the people I have had the pleasure to come across in this life, you alone have had the special impact to truly make a change in my life. The bond we have forged transcends time.
>
> . . . This Christmas I do not have a tangible gift for you. What I give you is my loyal friendship, my promise to be there for you and all of my prayers for you to have the best that God and life can possibly afford you. Simply put, I love you. Thank you for sharing me with yourself. It is quite a precious gift that I will treasure forever. God knew what he was doing when he put you down here. He radiates from you.
>
> Again let me state that throughout this life, no matter how far or not our paths diverge, I give you a piece of my heart and soul to carry with you until we meet again. Value it, hold it close, for not many receive such a gift—it is the hardest for me to give . . .

The Love Project not only allows many students to grow in developing their capacities for developing deep friendships but also breaks down barriers of age, social class, and culture.

LOVING THE ELDERLY

Many students developed substantial skills at relating to the elderly. One who had a strong aversion to older people because of negative feelings toward her grandmother worked through these feelings and developed a strong empathy and compassion not only for her grandmother but for elderly people in general. She often came and told me how difficult it was to attempt to overcome emotional barriers, but by the end of the semester she wrote in her journal, and told me, that it was one of the most meaningful experiences of her life.

Another told of relating to a man in his nineties who lived across the street from him and his friends. Before undertaking the project, my student had always assumed the man was annoyed at him and his fellow students, but the project revealed that the gentleman actually liked the young men and had often wished they would come over and talk with him. My student talked with his new elderly friend extensively and gained much wisdom and insight, as well as a great deal of warmth, from the relationship.

Numerous students regularly went to nearby nursing homes to visit elderly patients. Many reported feeling awkward and uneasy at first, not knowing what to say. However, with persistence, most were able to help their new friends come out of their shells. One student kept going back even though the lady she was relating to said next to nothing for the first several visits. Finally, the ice was broken and my student developed a warm, close, loving relationship with the lady, whose prior silence had been a defensive reaction against loneliness and the loss of her husband.

Another who persisted in trying to relate to a somewhat reclusive elderly lady but finally "broke through" and developed a close, warm relationship with her wrote:

> At first she was a little hesitant to really share anything with me since we had just met. It was beautiful though how after my second visit our relationship was growing. I had not expected anything from her really; I wanted to give some of myself to her. I took Buscaglia's advice to heart before I went: "One must endeavor to love all men even if he isn't loved by them. One doesn't love to be loved; he loves to love." She eventually did give love, the more we got to know each other. I also surprised myself with my ability to care for this woman in such a short time. She gave another dimension to life; this lady really had no one to share anything with, although she had a great deal of knowledge and wisdom to give to someone. She showed me a wonderful, simple, uncomplicated way of looking at life, and I hope she was able to capture a sparkle of youth through me.
>
> I learned new things about myself and interacting with other people. Learning about oneself is unending, and the help of others makes the learning easier. My experience will help me deal with others in the future and give me confidence to do so. Love is unlimited and unrestrained, it's a nonstop boat, everyone should come aboard.

One student wrote a very moving account of how he related to an eighty-year-old neighbor of his grandmother. At first he felt awkward and somewhat embarrassed in talking with her, but they quickly developed a deeply loving relationship. His feelings echoed those of many others who related to older people in their Love Projects:

> My grandmother wrote me one day and told me that what I was doing made such a difference in her neighbor's life. Her moods were much more cheerful, she wasn't as lonely, and most importantly it gave her things to look forward to other than dying. I was really proud of what I had done. I had really brought joy into someone else's life. I had also grown to fear becoming old a little bit less than I had before. I plan on stopping and seeing Mrs. Smith every time I am home. I have found love in a person whom I at one time stereotyped and looked down on. She has made my outlook on old people so much better that I am not afraid to approach anyone with gray hair and ask them a question. They need to feel needed. And simply asking someone elderly for advice on something brings so much joy into their lives. It doesn't have to be something of major importance; the important thing is that you ask and seek them out. I have found something that Leo Buscaglia says to be very true and that is that "love knows no age." Age had always been a barrier before I met Mrs. Smith. But if two people as different as we are can form a loving relationship then there is hope for anyone.

Several students stated that they had discovered a strong interest in working with the elderly they had previously not been aware of. Since Miami University has a strong program in gerontology through the Scripps Foundation, I was able to direct them to my colleagues Robert Atchley, Mildred Seltzer, and Sheila Miller to explore career possibilities in the field.

One student, Suzanne, described how the Love Project led to her vocational choice:

> This class has taught me more about myself and other people than any class I've ever taken. I've learned that I want to devote my life to helping people, especially older people. Through helping them, I help myself grow and become the person I want to become. I've also learned that at some point in my life I'm going to have to learn to accept death and accept what I have done in my life if I'm going to have any tranquillity and peace with myself. I've also learned to respect and delight in everyone's uniqueness, especially that of

older people. This may sound biased, but I think they are the most unique people of all because they have lived through the most experiences.

OVERCOMING SOCIAL CLASS
AND CULTURAL BARRIERS

As a sociologist, one of my specialties has been the study of social conflict and intergroup relations. I have often lectured on the causes of prejudice, racism, and conflict, but the Love Project provided many students with an opportunity not only to understand prejudice but to overcome it.

One student, for example, related to a Mexican student and developed a deep friendship after consciously trying, and succeeding, to overcome cultural boundaries and stereotypes. Since the substantial majority of the students come from white, upper-middle-class suburban backgrounds, the Love Project's success in helping them deal with and relate to people from very different cultural and social class backgrounds was one of the most heartening results. One student felt that she had gained not only a friend but something of lasting value:

> It made me think that some of the barriers people have built up against other people maybe aren't indestructible. We [she and the other members of her Love Group] weren't treating Juan as our "project" or as some poor soul we were good enough to help out. We treated him as our equal and as our friend. It's an experience like no other I've ever had and one that I would never trade. Even though I felt very uncomfortable at first, the benefits I got out of our project much outweighed this. It really helped me to grow as a person and understand the problems and similarities of seemingly totally different people.

> It's hard to believe that such a little part of myself can bring such a big return. It makes me want to invest more and more of myself. Relationships like this have really helped me to become a more loving person. And a better person. If I can continue in my love and acceptance of all people, I think I will truly become a happy and fulfilled person.

Another student related to a cook in his fraternity whom he and the other fraternity members had disliked. He developed a friendship across substantial social class lines and summarized his feelings about this:

> All in all I think my Love Project has been an incredible success. Ralph [the cook], for whom I had had little respect and didn't even know, has become a pretty good friend. I talk to him every afternoon after my classes. From what I can tell I think it provides a great release for him after a hard day's work. Just the other day I gave him a cigar because I knew he smokes them once in a while. I don't think anyone has ever done things like that for him. The great thing is, it makes me feel just as good as he does. It is a good way to illustrate how love is a two-way street. I'm very glad I have done this and that I decided on something as challenging as Ralph, who came from a completely different world than I did.

Another student took the time to get to know a mother on welfare and as a result gained a new appreciation of some of the aspects of many working-class people's lives she had previously been unaware of. During the semester, she came to witness and admire her new friend Barb's courage and perseverance trying to raise nine children without a husband and lacking good health:

> Now that my Love Project is "over" and I reflect on it, I have learned a great deal. I certainly hope it's not the end of the relationship, but I'm sure it's not. I have really evaluated and looked closely at my value system. When I observed Barb and her family and saw how much simple, key things meant to them, I couldn't help but get myself back into perspective. Maybe money, popularity, grades, success, etc. aren't all that important. Things like caring and family surely outrank or should outrank them. I felt like I was really getting materialistic—like, "Thank God, this project came just in time to save me from being exactly what I didn't want to become." But I can see the light now. I experienced love, a certain kind of love that I'll try my best to explain. I think that I received an unconditional love from Barb and her family, which in itself is very rare. But more than that, what I felt was different, too. It was meaningful and significant to love someone just for the sake of that caring and love, not for a reason or as reciprocal love. It was a new feeling for me from the beginning, that started as concern, grew to caring and love. As a friend and a (not to be too religious) sister in God's family. I don't know if that makes sense, but it's how I can best describe how I feel.
>
> The Love Project made me, well actually influenced me, to change

in several ways. First, I think that I will now accept people for who they are, not what they are or represent, because that can be and is often deceiving. Second, I have learned to look beyond what people dress like, or what kind of house they live in, or how much money they have. As I experienced, what is in someone's heart is so much more important. Third, and very importantly, I faced what it's like to be poor and to have real responsibilities that I've never dreamed of. The reality of not having everything you or your baby *needs,* not necessarily wants, is a harsh one. And I also learned how strong people have to be to deal with and accept these situations. Fourth, I've grown beyond my previous knowledge and potential. My former knowledge of the poor was little. Now I practically feel like a poor, less fortunate person when I'm there. It's like I'm humbled to a form of basic humanness or humaneness that I wish I could carry forever. My former potential (I refer to loving) has expanded because I never thought I could love someone who lived close to disgustingly and was so different from me. Well, needless to say, I turned out to be wrong. And fifth, I think that this experience will help me in any dealings that I'll ever have with people less fortunate than myself. I think that it takes a certain tact and yet caution in talking, and mostly the willingness to listen and learn.

I think it would be great if everyone took on a Love Project to bring some joy and caring to the poor, like I hope I did, because it's our responsibility as a society.

Julie, a junior in my Social Theory course who had already taken thirty-eight credit hours of psychology, was familiar with counseling techniques and the theory of the helping professions but felt something vital was missing in her training to that point. She was interested in applying the Love Project in the equivalent of a clinical setting. The results were so striking, and she expressed how she and her project person were transformed in such an eloquent way, that I will recount her Love Journal in full:

A few weeks ago my minister put me in contact with a twenty-six-year-old man from a neighboring church. This man, Mark, had just lost his wife and two children as a result of his wife- and child-battering rages. He was also on the verge of losing his job. As if this was not enough, he was forced to admit to his alcoholism and to seek treatment for that. He was not close to his family (parents and siblings) because, he said, they never really cared for him, and thus he could not turn to them for the love and support he so desperately needed. Though he had been close to his in-laws, they had turned bitter toward him because of what he had done to their daughter and grandchildren and family as a whole. My minister suggested I get acquainted with Mark and show him a little kindness and understanding. Hopefully my efforts would succeed in showing Mark a little light in that all-so-bleak tunnel.

One thing that needs mentioning here is that Mark and I could arrange only four meetings together before he had to leave to visit with his grandparents for a couple of months (in order to get away for a while). In view of this, we were forced to "jump right in" to the heart of the problem and work from there in a very short period of time.

Our first meeting was great. Everything went much better than I had expected. I expected things to be awkward and embarrassing; however, things were quite the contrary. I think things went so well because we both sort of knew each other prior to our meeting. My pastor told me of Mark's situation and likewise Mark was told everything about me—that I was doing a Love Project for college sociology. At first I wasn't sure if this was wise, but my pastor suggested it, so I agreed. Now, looking back, I know this was *essential* if we were to form any sort of a lasting friendship. I think it is necessary to lay all the cards on the table and then go from there and let things happen or not happen as you see it.

Our first meeting consisted of one drink (Pepsi) and some cookies followed by about five hours of *solid* communication. I found it incredibly easy to talk and listen to Mark, and he later told me that he has never gotten along with anyone else as well as he did with me! During this time we talked about his life and the things that he felt were responsible for his present situation. I knew most of the story prior to our meeting from my pastor; however, this did not spare me the sadness that I was going to feel as I was hearing of the situation firsthand.

Anyway, I learned a lot from Mark—a lot about people but especially a lot about love! I learned how important love is in one's life. I learned firsthand of all the terrible things people resort to because of feelings that they are unloved. During our conversations I talked to Mark about this project and about Buscaglia's *Love* book. I gave Mark my copy and after he read it, he told me that he would have given anything to have read that book fifteen years ago.

He told me something that almost made me cry—he told me that from the time he was old enough to remember, no one had ever told him that they loved him! Can you imagine this? A child being raised and never being told "I love you." After hearing things like this throughout our meetings, I was not surprised by anything that he told me he had done. As a matter of fact, I was surprised that he turned out as well as he did. Enough with all of this and on to the matter at hand—spouse and child abuse from the perspective of the *abuser*.

At first, I have to admit that I felt a little uneasy about meeting Mark. I had heard most of the background from my pastor and I have to admit that I put the blame mostly on Mark. However, this project has been an enlightening experience. Never before have I been forced to look at a situation from two perspectives objectively, especially concentrating on the perspective of the underdog. I must admit that I learned a valuable lesson, one which I'm sure will help me in the future when I can hopefully work as a counselor or social worker. I have learned to be objective and *listen*—there are always two sides and sometimes there can even be two *victims* such as in this case.

Background info: Mark was an only child until his father died and his mother remarried. Mark's new father—stepfather—had two children from a previous marriage, while Mark's mother and step-father had a child of their own. From the time Mark was eleven years old, he was expected—*forced*—to work in his stepfather's gas station from 4:30—right after school—until about 11 o'clock or midnight, seven days a week. Mark worked at the gas station eight or nine hours a day and he received no money for it either. He was expected to work to pay for his clothes, food, etc. Mark worked at this job until he was seventeen years old, when he left home.

One thing I learned of while talking to Mark that I was not aware of was that he attempted suicide when he was sixteen and was forced to seek psychiatric treatment for about six months. When I first talked to Mark he told me that he just didn't care anymore. At first I let this go, but after we got to talking a few more times, I asked him when he "stopped caring and gave up on life." He told me that it was when he started working in that gas station and realized all he was missing out on in life. He never got to go out, he never had friends, and he always got low grades in school because he was too tired to concentrate on his studies because he had worked eight hours the nights before.

As a result of this, Mark said his mother and stepfather called him names—"Stupid" and "Retard," etc. They told him that since he was dumb, he could never expect to do anything else but work in a gas station. Mark told me that the hardest thing to accept was the fact that he had to work while his peers—brothers and sisters— played, dated, participated in school activities. When I heard this I couldn't help but feel extremely sorry for Mark, and there is *no* way I could ever treat him mean or blame him for his present situation. Also, Mark said that he was physically as well as emotionally abused by his stepfather. One time Mark recalled he was ill and was sent home from school with a 103° fever. His father made him go to work that night. Mark said he remembered literally burning to death with fever; finally, he became so weak he passed out. His stepfather berated him when he awakened and told him to get back to work. After working a few minutes Mark was so dizzy that he gave a customer change for a twenty rather than a ten. At the end of the night when they were ten dollars off, his stepfather kicked him in the stomach, cracking two of his ribs. Mark says that all he remembers is the blood gushing out of his mouth and then waking up in the hospital. His stepfather, by the way, denied everything at the time and forced Mark to say that he got in a fight and was beaten up!

Our last meeting was filled with much emotion as we both attempted to put everything in proper perspective. This is the meeting that I will *always* remember. I think that I will be able to handle anything in my life as long as I remember the words that were spoken throughout the evening.

First, Mark and I talked about the previous meetings. He added things; I added things. Then he said something that literally broke my heart (in a good way). He told me that before I came into his life he had given up on everything—he had, to put it in his words, "hit rock bottom." However, he said that I showed him what life was really about. I showed him what love was all about and because of that he said that he had the will to go on. He realized that he had made some mistakes and that he had to rectify them, but for once in his life he really cared. He cared about himself—about his life and about *people.* He thanked me from the bottom of his heart and he said, "I love you. I love you because you gave me the one thing that I needed, the very thing which no one had ever given me— *love,* and with that I can take on whatever life has to offer." And lastly he said that for as long as he lived he would never forget me or the valuable lesson that I taught him. He said that he would be eternally grateful and that although he would never be able to repay me, he would always be willing to help me if I needed it. After he said that I told him that he had already repaid me and that he owed me nothing.

For our relationship served two purposes. First, it restored faith and love in his life and secondly, it showed me what life and love are all about. For the past two years I have been studying psychology and sociology with the intention of pursuing some kind of profession in social work, etc. But not until now, in this course, have I been able to grasp the true meaning of life. It is ironic but in all the psych courses (thirty-eight hours' worth) I can honestly say that I never learned anything half as meaningful as I have learned from the Love Project. I have seen with my own eyes what love can do for a person. As Buscaglia says, "Love is always the answer and with it man can change the world."

I have also seen what the lack of love can do—it can lead to many social evils such as crime, juvenile delinquency, drug abuse, spouse or child abuse, alcoholism, suicide. . . . Because of all this I feel that I can pursue my future with my "eyes open." With love I think I can help make this world a better place to be, if not for others at least for myself.

This project as well as my work at the battered wives shelter has helped me see the world from a different perspective. I have never experienced this kind of a life, like Mark's, and I have never been forced to try and understand or associate with people who have a life worse than I could ever imagine. I think that now I have sort of experienced a *rebirth*—I am not so naive about what is going on in the world. I realize that I have been extremely fortunate and I take every opportunity to thank God as well as my parents for that. I have definitely changed for the better as a result of this project—and I can honestly say that I like myself a hell of a lot better. Every time I think I have a problem I think about Mark and all those with similar or worse problems. I appreciate life and everything much more than before.

Since Mark has been in Houston, he has written me two letters to keep me informed as to what's happening in his life. As of yesterday Mark has made what seems to be remarkable progress. He is seeking counseling for his alcoholism as well as for his spouse battering. He said that he thinks just talking about *everything* has been the best medicine for all his pains. We are going to try and stay in touch, but even if we don't, somehow I know in my heart that everything will work out for him. He has what it takes to make something out of his life—love for himself and love for others around him!

I feel that this assignment has been the most inspirational endeavor I have ever attempted. I have learned truly what life and love are all about. For once I have been able to give someone something without ever expecting anything in return, although I got something I will always be grateful for. I know there are a lot of Marks out there in the world and I just hope that I will be able to help just a few more. It must be a wonderful experience going through life thinking you're a failure and everyone hates you—and then finding out that you can make something out of your life because people do care. Mark said it was the greatest thing that ever happened to him.

Violence begets violence. Clinical and other behavioral scientific studies of murderers and other violent people show clearly they were abused, usually severely, as children. In her book *For Your Own Good,* German psychiatrist Alice Miller (1982) discusses how abuse in childhood leads to violence in later life. A prime example of this is Adolf Hitler, who was severely beaten, sometimes nearly fatally, by his father. One can only imagine what might have happened had someone like Julie related to him in a loving manner while there was still time to counteract the overwhelming hatred and need for revenge that ultimately led to such terrible consequences for millions.

Julie's apparent success in helping Mark is reminiscent, on a smaller scale, of the work of Mahatma Gandhi, Dr. Martin Luther King, Jr., and others who have used love as a basic means of bringing about change.

As a sociologist, I am well aware that social problems have deep roots in social-structural, economic, and related "macrocosmic" factors. Love Projects are only small-scale efforts. Yet the success of Dr. King and others using love—in the sense of a deep respect and acceptance of one's adversaries' humanity—can and does have substantial results that often manage to avoid negative consequences of more conventional approaches to bringing about change.

Buscaglia makes it clear in his books and lectures that love is not just a feeling, but an action—an *active* orientation toward others, affirming them and oneself as well. People often confuse Agape with Eros, the type of love that rests on the desirable attributes of another and causes us to want to possess him or her.

In contrast, unconditional love is not just a feeling but an active affirmation of another, even if he or she has attributes we find negative, even disgusting. This type of love is part of the ideals of many of the major world religions. It is a particularly central part of the Christian tradition, although, as Buber's story of the rabbi illustrates (among many possible examples in many traditions), Agape is by no means limited to Christianity.

Some students, however, found their Christian faith enhanced substantially by the project. One stated she found deeper meaning in the biblical teachings to love others, realizing that "love is not necessarily an 'ooey-gooey' *feeling* but rather an *action*. The Love Project has been helpful to me in putting things together to form a complete picture. *Love* by Buscaglia and this project have made 'my picture' a more complete one. I sometimes get 'preachy' and I'm sorry if this gets to be 'too much.' It's just because I get excited though—I *love* to learn and see God work in people's lives."

Regardless of one's particular religious orientation or perspective, the universality of the transforming power of unconditional love is illustrated in a particularly moving account that involves a student, Brian, for whom "Love thy neighbor" took on new reality and meaning. His Love Journal is so touching that I will recount it in full.

> Over spring break I came to know a little boy next door who has a learning disability and comes from a family that, while sharing the same economic standards as mine, is different from us. Many of the concepts I have learned in class and read in the text and *Love* book relate to my experience with this little boy. Because of this experience, and the fact that I was given the opportunity to be involved in this through class, I have felt better about myself, have made a new friend, and have been given a unique educational experience different than I have ever encountered before.
>
> Before I relate my experience to you, I feel it is necessary to explain the circumstances surrounding it.
>
> I live in a middle-class suburb with all the trimmings—similar houses, nice streets, etc. More importantly, the people seem to be quite similar in regard to education, income, and life style. Because of this similarity, anything or anybody different is looked at in a negative way. Enter the new neighbors, who also happen to live right next door to me. They are, for want of a better term, "hillbillies" from the hills of West Virginia. I'm not quite sure how they were able to work their way out of the hills because neither the mother nor the father had much schooling. Needless to say, they

were quite different from anything my neighborhood had ever experienced.

The father played country music until the wee hours of the night; the mother just sat around until dinner, when she screamed her lungs out to round up the kids—one boy and two girls—who were always dirty, disrespectful of others' property, and in general a real nuisance. This is where my story really begins.

In the past, all the kids in the neighborhood, myself included, ridiculed and were downright cruel to the three kids, who were younger than us, never bothering to get to know them. We would scare them by pretending to run them over with our bikes and exclude them from any games or activities we had. This past spring break, I was not able to go to Florida, but instead had to go home. I dreaded a week of nothing to do because all my friends either work, or are away at school, or were in Florida.

On Tuesday of that week, my whole attitude changed. I was pulling weeds in my mom's flower bed when I noticed the little boy from next door, whom I will call Joey, watching me and, as usual, he asked if he could help. I said no, that he didn't have to, because I knew if I said yes, he would bother me the rest of the day. A little later, when I had finished, I noticed Joey sitting in his driveway and I felt something I had never felt for him before—genuine compassion and the urge to reach out and tell him I was sorry for all the cruel things my friends and I had done to him a couple of years before. I don't know exactly why I all of a sudden felt this way, but I think it was in part maturity and in part some of the things I learned in this class about love. I asked him if he would like to play catch. He really had never played before but didn't lack enthusiasm. We played for about an hour the first day. On Wednesday I actually looked forward to seeing him and when I did, I gave him an old mitt and hat from my Little League days. He was overjoyed and seemed to have a never-ending source of energy. This went on for a week, and although he is not the best baseball player in the world, we both got a very important thing from that week—a new friend.

When I got back here to school, I tried to think of why for all those years I had never liked Joey without ever really knowing him. The reason lay in concepts I have learned in this class. Joey's family had grown up in a very different atmosphere than any of my neighbors or my family. This means they went through a different process of socialization, which in turn led to different values and norms, such as child rearing, family life, amount of education, and sexual attitudes, than my parents and other neighbors had. These differences caused my parents as well as my friends' parents to not be as friendly to the new neighbors as they would have to people with similar backgrounds. This unfriendly attitude was passed on to us, and in turn, we treated the new kids in the way that we did. The new family also is an example of another sociological factor, vertical mobility. They experienced the same problems as, let's say, a black family moving from the ghettos to my neighborhood. These factors help me now understand why all the people in my neighborhood, especially the kids, treated Joey's family the way they did.

The reason I reached out to Joey at that moment didn't have anything to do with those sociological factors but with love. The passage from Buscaglia's *Love* book which I can pinpoint being the biggest influence on me at that time was his statement that real love creates rather than destroys. I, along with Joey, created a friendship. I reached out and he responded, and if we were to never see each other again, we would always hold fond memories of that week and our friendship we created. I can honestly say I have learned something that will stay with me as long as I live.

A year after I had first assigned the Love Project, I sent follow-up questionnaires to assess its lasting effects. Of the twenty-nine who responded, a very substantial majority indicated continued positive effects (17 percent strong, 66 percent some continued effects). Only 3 percent said there was very little continuing effect, the remainder indicating continued increases in desire to help others, compassion for others, and similar love-related patterns (see Table 4).

Although the Love Project had no specific religious and a very generalized spiritual content, lesser, but still significant, change was apparent in religious and spiritual perspectives, such as religious feelings, belief in a higher power, and inner sense of God's presence. Interestingly, 28 percent of the follow-up respondents indicated some decrease in fear of death, even though the project (with the exception of limited discussion of NDEs) was very life-oriented. However, in contrast to most NDErs, desire for material things declined in only a small portion (24 percent overall) of my Love Project students.

Overall, the Love Project affected many students' lives, some apparently quite profoundly, as an anonymous student's comment on the year-later questionnaire illustrates:

> I have changed a lot toward other people, and this project is what made me change. I looked at people in terms of classes, races, col-

ors, and "types," and I'm glad to say that I don't do this as much anymore. I look at people as human beings now, and before I don't really know if I was doing this. I can honestly say life is much more fun, interesting, beautiful, and enjoyable now that I see people and the world in a different perspective. It is now no longer boring, or the same old routine. I have changed mostly in the fact that I now want to help others. I'm more aware of people's feelings, even if they are different from mine. Life is easier to live and go through because I feel I understand many aspects of life that I know I experienced but really didn't realize any significance of before. I'm finding I'm willing to go out of my way for people I normally wouldn't have gone out of my way for before the Project (but I enjoy doing it, for I've learned the true meaning of love in giving of yourself, even if rejected). This will stay with me the rest of my life.

TRANSCENDING "SUPERIORITY" AND "INFERIORITY"

Before the Love Project, Brian saw Joey as "lower" than himself. This attitude reflects an outmoded world view that places people "higher" and "lower" than one another not only socially but in terms of their supposed superiority and inferiority. NDErs, and many of my Love Project students, have a new world view in which they are able not only to recognize but to relate to the essence and ultimate worth of themselves and others, as did my student Stephanie, who worked with delinquent children:

> Looking back over the experience of the Love Project fills me with a special feeling. I feel I grew and helped others grow in the process.
>
> How did I benefit? I learned that I was an extremely valuable person just for myself. I didn't have to give anything to the boys except for my love and attention, and that was all they needed. I was accepted unconditionally and discovered that I could accept them without restrictions either. To me, they weren't delinquents or outcasts; they were my friends. I learned to reject labels; they have no meaning or place in our society. I found I could reach out to people in situations that I had not thought possible. I'm basically shy, but the meaningful interactions I experienced with the boys has helped me overcome that. The Love Project has helped me restore my faith in

humanity. Giving and caring is a totally rewarding experience, and would be the answer to all our problems if people would just take the time to give it a chance.

But is this "realistic?" What about the greatest social problem of all—war? Might the NDE, and such efforts as the Love Project, and other kinds of unconditional love, help develop new ways of overcoming war?

WAR AND THE NDE:
TWO SIDES OF THE
COIN OF HUMAN EXISTENCE

As many people, echoing such writers as Jonathan Schell (1982), stress, we are living precariously at a time when immortality itself, in the "earthly" sense of not having any future children to carry on humanity, is threatened. In what ways might the NDE help overcome the greatest threat to human existence, which, as many have noted, must be overcome if it is not to overcome us?

There is a curious similarity between war and the NDE. War confronts the basic issues of life and death. In a televised PBS interview conducted by producer Nancy Roberts dealing with Vietnam veterans entitled "Now Tell Us All about the War," author Philip Caputo talked about his combat experiences:

> It was literally as though a door to hell had been opened, and I then stuck my head in and saw what was going on there. And then the door closed, and I was back in ordinary life again. . . .

> When a man goes into combat, as a very young man, he is killed and reborn into something else. That experience is as transforming as the experience of birth itself. It was and always will remain the major event of my life until I die. Nothing will ever supersede it.

Interestingly, *NDErs say exactly the same things about their experiences—with the central, basic difference that the NDE opens up to them the "doors of heaven."* The NDE and war are thus, in an intriguing way, two sides of the coin of life and death, heaven and hell, positive and negative—in Freud's terms, Eros, the "life instinct," and Thanatos, the death instinct.

This suggests that the NDE may have the capacity to serve as a seedbed for the emergence of new kinds of *functional equivalents* of war, in ways basically similar to those that William James, in his famous essay (1911) saw as the possibilities of a "moral equivalent of war." As the Love Project students found, it takes discipline, effort, and even courage to help others. Perhaps such efforts might provide the same sort of confrontation with the forces of life and death, particularly if they involve working with the elderly, the terminally ill, and others facing death, that war now provides. Certainly, the close love and comradeship and the genuine "I-Thou" relationships soldiers in combat cite as a prime essence of their wartime experiences are also central to the NDE and to Love Project encounters. The fact that the NDE is the life-affirming "heads" side of the coin of life and death of which war and combat are the death-dealing "tails" side is an intriguing phenomenon that may prove very useful in terms of finding new ways to deal with and overcome war.

Countless youths have sacrificed their lives on the altar of military glory. One of the central ironies of human existence is the mythology of war, which promises eternal life with death in battle.

Many cultures focus on the glory of sacrificing oneself in battle. The Japanese kamikaze pilots and human torpedos fervently believed they were achieving immortality by dying for the emperor. The leader or the cause becomes the locus, in Becker's view (1975), of immortality power. Ironically, the cost of life is death.

Is there any way out of this dilemma? Does meaning in life always have to come at the expense of one's own, or others', lives, either literally as in war or symbolically in the thousand little deaths people die each day trying to achieve meaning and purpose by a futile search for some supposedly meaningful immortality vehicle such as money, power, or fame? Even sacrifice for the sake of ideals often ends up negating and reversing the ideals for which the sacrifices were made.

Both the NDE and the Love Project emphasize that true meaning and fulfillment come not at someone else's expense but through a genuine Agape in which one's own fulfillment is the same as fulfilling the other. Human beings are continually trying to gain "success" seeking fulfillment in something less than the ultimate law of God's eternal love. When the ultimate is conceived, as it is in the NDE, as total love, there need be no breach between the *means* of gaining immortality (loving and serving others) and the *end* of mutual meaning and immortality.

Though this may sound abstract, a moment's reflection will reveal that, in fact, it is a pervasive perception throughout our own and probably many other cultures. A colleague of mine recently died an untimely death at the age of forty-four of Lou Gehrig's disease. A person with many friends, she had spent much time helping learning-disabled students, outside of class, to write more effectively. In the obituaries, our provost mentioned that he would always remember her work with these students, as I'm sure the students themselves will.

When all is said and done, we judge people, in the final analysis, not by the criteria of positions, degrees, titles, and other manifestations of "success," but by *what they have done for others*. The NDE, and by extension the Love Project and countless similar informal and formal endeavors, incorporates this truth and affirms that, indeed, giving love to others is sufficiently important, not only in the sense of how others will remember us, but *eternally*. As the experience shows, we empathically experience the effects and consequences of our action on others, and the stuff of heaven is thus an extension of the joy and satisfaction we obtain when we know we have affected others positively through the love we have allowed to be channeled through us to them.

In our era, one of the best-known and most effective exemplars of this law of love was the Reverend Martin Luther King, Jr. King, like other leaders past and present who have had substantial impacts on history as well as other individuals, saw humanity moving toward a "beloved community" in which humanity would be united in love (Ansbro, 1984). Incorporating Reinhold Niebuhr's awareness that Agape on the individual level is not sufficient to bring about a total transformation because love must always be transformed into justice in the social context, King inspiringly set forth a vision of a time when "Jews and Gentiles, Protestants and Catholics, the sons and daughters of slaves and former salve-owners, will unite in brotherhood." In his last sermon, he stated he didn't want people to emphasize the prizes and honors he had obtained but said that he had "tried to give his life serving others . . . tried to love somebody." And in the last speech he gave, the night before his death, he proclaimed an NDE-like prophetic vision.

> We've got some difficult days ahead. But it really doesn't matter with me now. Because I've been to the mountaintop. I don't mind. Like anybody, I would like to live a long life—longevity has its place. But I'm not concerned about that now. I just want to do God's will. And He's allowed me to go up to the mountain. And I've looked over, and I've *seen* the Promised Land. I may not get there with you. But I want you to know tonight that we as a people will get to the Promised Land. So I'm happy tonight, I'm not worried

about anything, I'm not fearing any man—mine eyes have seen the glory of the coming of the Lord!

It would be wrong, however, to assume that the NDE or its equivalents, such as Dr. King's vision or endeavors like the Love Project, it might constitute a fulfillment of history without negative potentialities. As Reinhold Niebuhr (1953) warns, every new human potentiality contains the capacity for evil as well as good. NDErs, for example, can misuse their psychic powers, and some of the less well adjusted of them have done so by setting themselves on a "spiritual pedestal" and telling others things about them that have proven harmful, thus allowing (as Tom Sawyer puts it) "greed and ego" to transcend the Light's imperative of love. Others may see the NDE, the Love Project, and the unconditional love they promulgate as leading to the perfectibility of humanity, without realizing that every form of progress, including moral progress, is fraught with the perils of human limitations. As I have pointed out, NDErs are human and should not be regarded as sanctified because of their experience.

The essence of the NDE is, of course, nothing basically new. Rather, it is a *reaffirmation* in a particularly dramatic and, insofar as it is a byproduct of advanced biomedical technology, a new way, of what the world's great religions have been telling us all along. In the Christian tradition, this message can be found throughout the New Testament, in the light referred to in the opening verses of the Gospel of John. This light came into the world and was experienced not only by the Apostles but by many subsequently, such as Saint Augustine, who in his *Confessions* describes his soul's ascent to God in a way very reminiscent of NDErs' descriptions of their experiences:

> . . . And I . . . beheld with the eye of my soul, above my mind, the Light Unchangeable. Not this ordinary light, which all flesh may look upon, nor as it were a greater of the same kind, as though the brightness of this should be manifold brighter, and with its greatness take up all space. Not such was this light, but other, yea, far other from all these. Nor was it above my soul, as oil is above water, nor yet as heaven above earth; but above to my soul, because It made me; and I below It, because I was made by It. He that knows the Truth, knows what that Light is; and he that knows It, knows eternity. Love knoweth it. O Truth Who art Eternity! and Love who are Truth! and Eternity Who art Love! (VII, 10.16-17.23; trans. E. B. Pusey [Oxford: 1838])

11

Living in the Light

"To lose the earth you know, for greater knowing; to lose the life you have, for greater life; to leave the friends you loved, for greater loving; to find a land more kind than home, more large than earth—

"—Whereon the pillars of this earth are founded, toward which the conscience of the world is tending—a wind is rising, and the rivers flow."

Thomas Wolfe, *You Can't Go Home Again*

The title of Thomas Wolfe's last book refers to the home of childhood, the place where one first encounters life and its struggles and triumphs. But even if one can't return to this earthly home, we can all return to our true home. This is a basic message of the NDE.

Is it possible that humanity may yet find a home on earth, free from the travails of cruelty, poverty, alienation, and all the other ills that cause us to dream of a Kingdom of God on earth? The NDE and the Love Project show that such a kingdom already exists. It is all around us, not in the form of political systems or ideologies but within us, and in the small but universally and ultimately significant acts of kindness, compassion, and love that are the marrow and meaning of our existence. It is in this recognition, and in allowing ourselves to be instruments of the Light, that we arrive at our true destiny and our true home.

Human beings have never felt fully at home on earth. Our "creatureliness" contrasts with our spirit. Many view belief in an afterlife as illusory. Yet, as Niebuhr points out (1953), it is even more illusory to imagine that anything short of God's grace can bridge the gap between human temporality and eternity. To assume otherwise is to form ideologies and visions that, when they inevitably fall short, require the sacrifice of scapegoats.

Far from constituting an illusion, the assumption of an afterlife—in the sense in which it is conveyed by the NDE, with the love of the Light as central—allows for the completion of the meaning of both individual lives and history. It also (assuming it is seen as the NDEr conceives it, as involving the total love and knowledge of the light) avoids the perils of perfectionist ideologies, which assume that ideal new orders or classless societies can and should be realized on earth. All such dreams call for sacrifice—of the present for the sake of the future, of one class for the sake of the triumph of another, or of one race at the expense of "lower" races. Those who believe themselves to be in possession of the "final truth" thus make the earth a home neither for themselves nor for others, because their own genuine fulfillment is inevitably compromised by the suppression and, in the final but not uncommon consequence, elimination of those whose deaths provide the basis of the illusory gain of immortality.

For Christians, the Cross is the sacrifice to end the need for sacrifices. The Resurrection, moreover, is the complete triumph over death and sin that allows us to be free from the need for immortality striving and frees us to overcome everything that blocks the fulfillment of our capacity to love. And, most importantly, the forgiveness and unconditional love provided us through this sacrifice enables us to accept and love ourselves and thus to fulfill the supreme commandment to "Love God with all our hearts, minds, and strength, and our neighbor as ourselves." Mother Teresa, Martin Luther King, and countless others have fulfilled this promise, in their own lives and for others.

Human societies, including of course nominally "Christian" ones, are still based largely on judgmental and sacrifical immortality systems in which one's worthiness rests on how well he or she conforms to social values or norms, either through inborn traits such as appearance or through effort. The NDE, conveying the deepest message of the greatest religious traditions, does away with such conditions and renders the infinite love of God actualizable in and through the smallest acts of kindness and compassion of finite human beings. *Every act of kindness and compassion reverberates throughout humanity.* Each human being—man, woman, or child, the rich and the poor, famous or obscure, owner or worker—shares the gift and blessing of doing good. It is not necessary to be wealthy to do good for others, as NDErs, my Love Project students, and countless others past and present have shown. Money may help, but money doesn't do all. Being a channel for God's unconditional love requires earnest purpose, honest self-devotion, and hard work. Relate to others in a loving way, and especially the disadvantaged, distressed, and helpless—the poor, the elderly and widowed, unloved children, the sick, the "deviant" person—for the sake of our shared humanity. In particular, help all who are suffering; this need not be "unrealistic" but can be done for one's daily work in the newly emerging service society as a basis for providing for oneself and one's family. Work in this way will lead to genuine honor, as Mickey Staccato realized, and the genuine "fame" of others knowing that you have allowed the love of the Light to affect their lives. In this way, your fulfillment comes *through,* not at the expense of, others' fulfillment.

This is true not only in an idealistic context but in the hardheaded world of business. Peters and Waterman (1982) examined numerous highly successful companies. Using Ernest Becker's mode of analysis as an important dimension of their approach, they found that the employees of the successful companies had a strong sense of meaning and purpose in their work. Moreover, this sense of purpose was strongly related to the successful companies' strong emphasis on service to customers. Allman (1984) discusses experimental evidence that shows that cooperation and "being nice" pays off. *Helping others is, ultimately, helping oneself,* now and eternally.

The ideal of love is applicable to all aspects of life. In the last analysis, people freed from the fear of death and of others become motivated to do things by love. Each and every truly creative endeavor—artistic, entrepreneurial, or charitable—that flows through us once we are free from immortality striving is a Love Project. We must allow the love of the Light to operate in and through our talents and capacities, trusting in its deepest directives. In Joe Geraci's words:

> I believe love can be just as infectious as hate. It has to turn around. And to do that, people have to start somewhere. On a small scale, just me telling you about my experience, and someone reading what you're going to write. It multiplies quickly. And I'm not the only one has had this experience. There are thousands of us all around the world. Multiply my story by a thousand and you'll see how quickly it can grow! It can be done. In fact, it has already started. (Quoted by Taylor, 1981)

The kind of love Joe and other NDErs, as well as many people who have never had transcendental experiences, seek to know is not a selfish love based on one's own or others' special characteristics, but an unconditional *agape* that we are not the source of, but which we receive as a gracious gift from God and give freely to others. As John White puts it,

> The world's great spiritual systems . . . understand the psychology of this situation very well, and have developed procedures for curing it by disburdening people of their false self-image, their false identity. It is no accident that society's models of the God-realized human being, the self-actualized person, include many saints and holy people. They have been revered for many reasons: their compassion, devotion and serenity, their inspirational words of wisdom, their service to the world. What has been their motivation?

Each of them, in his/her own way, arising from particular culture or tradition, has discovered the secret of the ages, the truth of the saying, "Let go and let God." When the ego sense is relaxed, when a sense of the infinite and eternal replaces our usual narrow self-centeredness with all its passing, unsatisfying fantasies, there is no longer a mental basis for fear, hatred, anxiety, anger, attachment, desire. Instead, the perfectly harmonious functioning of the cosmos operates through us—and the cosmos is always in balance, always at peace with itself. (1981 b:44)

Christ, in White's view, is the epitome of this, and our task is to emulate him, to move toward a higher state of humanity in which, freed from the fear of death, we are free to love ourselves and each other unconditionally. Christ wanted people to follow him, to develop the same kind of love toward others He showed to them. In John White's words:

. . . Jesus was aware of himself as a finished specimen of the new humanity which is to come—the new humanity which is to inherit the earth, establish the Kingdom, usher in the New Age. . . . His unique place in history is based upon his unprecedented realization of the higher intelligence, the divinity, the Ground of Being incarnated in him—the ground which is the source of all Becoming. . . . He called us to *follow* him, to follow in his steps, to learn from him, from his example. He called us to share in a new condition, to enter a new world, to be one in the supramental Christ consciousness which alone can dispel the darkness of our minds and renew our lives. (1981a:15)

The importance of obeying Christ's teachings to love God with all one's heart, mind, and strength and to love one's neighbor as oneself was the central lesson of the Love Project of one of my students, a devout Christian:

This Project definitely had an impact on my life. God has directly spoken to me through some of the things I've learned as I've tried to love [others]. . . . I see that love is an *action*—a *choice* we make. Sure, there are times when I honestly *feel* love but I can't live by or count on those feelings. That is one of the main things that God has enforced on my heart through this Love Project.

. . . Love is not just an emotion, or even an action, as I've said. *Love is God.* Love is eternal. Love is powerful. Love is the *only* thing that can save the human race from eternal separation from God. There-

fore, love is not something to put aside when I'm not feeling particularly loving or willful. We are commanded to love one another fervently!

I'm *finally* seeing that God doesn't put things in the Bible because
they sound nice—He means it! The fact that I've been assigned this
Love Project at the same time I've been assigned to study 1 Peter is
no mistake—all things happen for a reason. It has been *so* valuable
for me to practically see and apply the things I've been studying in
the Bible.

The way of practical application leads me to Leo Buscaglia's idea
that *love is learned.* I have learned from this viewpoint of his! The
way to learn is to *do!* Also, he talks about learning by example. I
learned all these things and have been able to apply them by doing
my Love Project.

First of all, I have seen that I need to *practice* love. I cannot expect
to "love" someone once and have it mastered. But rather, I need to
love over and over—during the good times and the bad—realizing
I'll always need to *grow* in love. . . . The more we step out and
love—the more we practice it—the more it becomes a habit. Yet
I've also grown in my ability to *love by choice* (denying self). On
those days when I didn't *feel* like loving—when I want to think
more of myself than others I've grown in my realization that we
need to *live* our faith—by *loving.* It's much easier to go up to a
perfect stranger and share the Gospel with him—and then walk
away to never see him again. But to personally invest myself into
another's life—to commit myself to *do* something time and
again—*takes effort.* Sometimes, I honestly would rather not bother
to love others. What I want is not nearly as important as the *fact*
that people need to *see* and experience the love of Jesus through
others *letting* Him live freely through them. Jesus put no time limits or depth limits on His love. We celebrate Easter tomorrow because He literally poured Himself out for us on the Cross. We all
have different gifts to be used for the building up of the body of
Christ. Yet we *all* have love (Jesus) and "the greatest of these is
love." Ephesians 4 talks about the body of Christ and how we need
to *liberally* use our gifts for the eventual unification of the body of
Christ to glory Him. We each have a part of God (and His love)
within us—all *combined* we can make *One BIG GOD!* Therefore,
the free expression of that love is planned, needed, and necessary. It
[love] was given to us as a gift, so it is not ours to hoard. Through
the Love Project, I've had to love by choice many times. I've conse-
quently had the above point driven home. My choosing is not just a

personal accomplishment, but *necessary* for fulfilling God's purpose.

Lastly, I must honestly say that my experiences with the Love Project (the learning, the practice, etc.) have in part been responsible for an increased *feeling* of love. Even though I feel we should not depend on feelings, we cannot deny them either. Emotions are good when taken as God wants them to be. After all, he made us and *gave* us emotions. I have grown in my compassion and am more able to be affectionate with *others* in my life besides my Love Project person.

The NDE, and many Love Project experiences and their equivalents, break down hierarchic imageries and allow people to see the innate unity of all people and things without social or cultural (e.g., age, sex, class; "advanced" vs. "less advanced" peoples) prejudices. Rather than seeing God as separated from us by space or by time, God is perceived as One and in all, the Universal Christ overcoming all separation between I and Thou.

The Love Project represents and tries to promulgate compassion based on the ultimate worth of each human being. It is, in this sense, a recapitualization of the NDE, in its deepest meaning if not in terms of what Love Project people (and anyone who engages in any Agape activity) actually undergo. God's love is thus not just some mere abstraction, but is rather *actualized in the love that exists between people* who relate to one another in an I-Thou relationship, in which *the deepest part of each human being recognizes, affirms, and actualizes the God and the Christ in the other.* This is the essence of Mother Teresa's relating to each of the destitute sick and suffering people she helps, whom she regards—each and every one—as Christ. It is also the essence of Martin Luther King's approach which stresses the ultimate worth of each human being despite his or her prejudices or views, which may lead him or her toward aggression and even brutality; no matter what evil a person does, this does not constitute the *essence* of the person, in the ultimate sense. It is this recognition that is at the heart of Agape, of NDEs and of the kinds of ideals that are actualized day in and day out in countless ways as an *infrastructure* of the Kingdom of God on earth.

Exercises such as the Love Project, based on Buscaglia's ideas and the central teachings of the world's religions, can be an important way of realizing and actualizing this. In the words of my student Suzanne:

This is the second Love Project I have done. The first one introduced me to the potentialities of helping people and this one has
instilled me with certainty as to my future. It's easy to read and
accept Buscaglia's ideas. But you won't understand them until you
live and experience human love and uniqueness. Only then can you
truly begin to fathom the infinite amount of senses and love
rhythms in each human spirit. We, as a society, have discovered
our evil side; now it is time to discover our good side. We must
open peoples' minds and souls, that strive for immortality, to the
teachings of Love. And then the fragile bud will blossom into an
everlasting world of united, brotherly peoples.

In the Christian vision, this brother-and-sisterhood will arrive when
people realize that they are free not only from death, but free to love
God, each other, and themselves without fear or guilt because they have
been forgiven by ". . . the one God and the one mediator between man
and God, the man Christ Jesus, who gave his life as a ransom for all." (I
Timothy 2:5-6 NIV).

Each person's love multiplies, and the unity of all that had existed
all along is finally realized in a Kingdom of God ". . . on earth, as it is in
Heaven."

The end of the prize-winning film *Places in the Heart* epitomizes
this, according to NDErs I've talked with who have seen it. Throughout
most of the film, the characters have hurt and abused one another in
various ways: A young black man has accidentally killed a sheriff and is,
in turn, lynched; a man cheats on and hurts both his wife and his lover;
Ku Klux Klan members beat up another black; a banker nearly causes a
widow to lose her home. Yet, in the end, during a Communion service
in which 1 Corinthians 13 ("Love is patient, love is kind") is recited,
all—including some who have died—are reconciled with one another in
forgiveness, unity, and love. NDErs gain a similar vision in their experiences, and its actualization in a fulfillment of the Kingdom of God on
earth is at the heart of the ultimate meaning not only of the NDE but of
the sort of world all humanity strives to attain. It is a vision of a world in
which "love is the only axiom."

Human beings are dear to one another. Everyone desires, deep
down, to help others, to be the conveyer of blessings, no matter how
small, to others, to be kind to those who need kindness, for the sake of
that which we all share and for the love of the Light we can all convey.
At the root of our nature, and of the universe, is one Light, and through
it, One Human Heart. As Eberhard Arnold, founder of the Bruderhof,

stated, "You only have to go back far enough. In the ultimate depths, everything good and true that men have ever known, thought or lived, comes from the one source of light. Our vocation is to make the way free for it." (1964:36).

Kevin Krupp summarized his Love Project:

Is it possible for everyone in the world to become more loving, to pull themselves away from those inhibitions or institutions that keep them from doing so? I can speak for myself that it is possible.

I was inspired by a sunset in Florida over spring break. A storm had just ended and the sun cracked between the clouds and the earth, making fire of the clouds and a mirror of the water. I tried to create a powerful statement that would inspire other people into making the best of their lives with other people. It went like this:

> If I can make a difference in the world today,
> Affecting the lives of those around me,
> Washing their shores with the water of my life,
> Let me storm the earth with my potential,
> Giving all I have
> Until the sun sets.

Afterword
Kenneth Ring, Ph.D.
author of
Life at Death and
Heading toward Omega

Man's path is not only forward, but also upward; not only into the future, but also toward the light.

The natural religion of mankind is revealed through the instincts to love, to hope and to serve. When these generous impulses direct human activities, humanity is one congregation united in truth rather than by allegiance to a name.

Charity in the sense of generosity to the poor or the afflicted . . . is to be understood only as an expression of, or an action impelled by, the internal experience of the mystery of love.

Most persons achieve this quality in the silence of their own hearts, but once they have known it they are united as one person in the love of God and dedicated as one person in the service of good.

—Manly P. Hall, *The Mystical Christ*

In *After the Beyond,* Chuck Flynn has offered us a moving, testimony-filled delineation of what Manly P. Hall has described as "the natural religion of mankind." This religion of no name is born through a direct *experiential* realization, not just a belief in, God's perfect love; it expresses itself *naturally* and grows through loving service to others. In this book NDErs, especially those who have encountered the Light and have felt its love engulf them, are shown to be persons who infuse a new energy into this timeless religion about which Saint Augustine himself said that it always had exacted, with the death of Jesus Christ, came to be called Christianity. Thus the NDErs whose accounts dominate this book bring no *new* message to us—their song of love, though ancient, has its origins not in history but in the human heart—yet they have burst forth into the drama of contemporary life with a force and seeming ubiquity that compels our attention. Just what is the source of our now decade-long fascination with these so-called Near-Death Experiences? They are no longer "news"—most people have heard of them by now—but our absorption with them remains. Why?

There are, to be sure, many reasons to be drawn to these experiences, for they speak to the perennial longings—and fears—of humanity, and they appear to provide profound insights into matters for which all religions exist to supply an answer. Yet beyond these powerful concerns, there is, I think, an additional source of interest that has to do with the perceived *timeliness* of these revelations. Why is it, one may ask, that at this point in humanity's troubled history we are being flooded with countless firsthand descriptions of death that at once strip it of its fearfulness and divulge the importance of living—or attempting to live—in selfless love and compassionate understanding? As Chuck Flynn has observed, millions of adults, just in the United States alone, have already had NDEs; resuscitation technology guarantees that many millions more, *around the world,* will have this experience in the future. *After the Beyond* demonstrates how people—even pretty "unsavory" people by conventional social and moral standards—tend to be transformed by their NDEs; and other research, published and yet to appear, reinforces Chuck's data and upholds the conclusions of his book.

Clearly, something of note is happening—something big; something on a planetary scale; and something that seems to have the power to make us, as Hall says, "one congregation united in truth." Something universal is surfacing in our time and is surfacing fast, as though there is a certain urgency that it be *noticed* and acted upon swiftly. NDEs are not simply stories; they are teachings and teachings with a particular relevance *now.* And the transformations to which NDEs lead are not just individually uplifting; they seem to prefigure something in our *collective* future, the first indications of which are already apparent.

I am suggesting, of course, that others besides myself who are more than casually interested in the NDE as a phenomenon sense, whether dimly and inchoately or openly and explicitly, some such larger meaning in this. In *Heading toward Omega,* for example, I propose that NDEs may point to the next stage of human evolution, and the response that that hypothesis has already evoked convinces me that I am far from alone in holding that view. Reading Chuck Flynn's beautiful book shows me that he, too, endorses a similar interpretation. In Chuck's case, however, I believe that by emphasizing endeavors such as the Love Project he is saying something more, namely, that we should not simply *wait* for the coming of Omega, so to speak, but should participate actively in its emergence.

In the framework that Chuck and I share, though, the NDE is potentially a powerful source of humanity's regeneration and evolution; and the Love Project is nothing else but life lived in harmony with the truth each of us already contains within to which NDErs serve so forcibly to resensitize us. In this important and timely book, then, Chuck Flynn is asking us not only to ponder the implications of NDEs and their transformative effects but to *act* upon these implications by, as it were, designing our own Love Project. In this way, we can all participate consciously in the awakening of humanity to its own divinity and speed the day when we shall all more radiantly reflect the Light in our daily lives on planet Earth.

Tables

TABLE 1: ATTITUDE AND VALUE CHANGES AMONG NDErs (N=21)

	% Increase		% No	% Decrease	
	Strong	Some	Change	Some	Strong
Concern for Others					
Desire to help others	72	14	14	0	0
Compassion for others	76	19	5	0	0
Ability to listen patiently to others	71	14	10	5	0
Tolerance for others	57	24	19	0	0
Ability to express love openly to others	67	19	14	0	0
Insight into others' problems	52	29	19	0	0
Understanding of others	48	42	10	0	0
Acceptance of others	67	19	14	0	0
Death-Related Attitudes					
Fear of death	0	0	0	14	86
Belief in an afterlife	90	5	5	0	0
Spirituality and Religion					
Belief that life has inner meaning	95	0	5	0	0
Feeling of the inner presence of God	71	24	5	0	0
Religious feelings	52	33	10	5	0
Interest in sacred things	67	19	14	0	0
Tendency to pray	38	42	10	10	0
Interest in organized religion	14	29	29	10	18
Materialism					
Concern with material things	0	0	29	33	38
Desire for wealth	0	0	48	24	29

TABLE 2: ATTITUDE AND VALUE CHANGES
        AMONG Non-NDE SURVIVORS (N=12)

	% Increase		% No	% Decrease	
	Strong	Some	Change	Some	Strong
Concern for Others					
Desire to help others	42	25	33	0	0
Compassion for others	33	42	25	0	0
Ability to listen patiently to others	33	17	33	8	8
Tolerance for others	8	42	42	0	8
Ability to express love openly to others	25	25	33	8	8
Insight into others' problems	42	33	25	0	0
Understanding of others	42	33	25	0	0
Acceptance of others	0	25	58	8	8
Death-Related Attitudes					
Fear of death	8	25	25	16	25
Belief in afterlife	16	8	67	0	8
Spirituality and Religion					
Belief that life has inner meaning	16	42	16	16	8
Feeling of the inner presence of God	25	50	16	0	8
Religious feelings	25	25	42	0	8
Belief in Higher Power	25	33	33	0	8
Tendency to pray	42	8	42	0	8
Interest in organized religion	16	33	42	0	8
Materialism					
Concern for material things	0	16	33	25	25
Desire for wealth	0	16	50	16	16

TABLE 3: ATTITUDE, VALUE, AND PERSONAL GROWTH
CHANGES AMONG LOVE PROJECT PARTICIPANTS
AT END OF COURSE (N=428)

	% Increase		% No	% Decrease	
	Strong	Some	Change	Some	Strong
Concern for Others					
Desire to help others	20	62	17	0	0
Compassion for others	20	62	16	1	0
Ability to listen patiently to others	21	62	16	1	0
Tolerance for others	34	50	15	1	0
Ability to express love openly to others	15	58	27	1	0
Insight into the problems of others	20	67	13	1	0
Understanding of others	18	67	13	2	1
Acceptance of others	21	65	12	2	1
Personal Growth					
Feelings of self-worth and self-esteem	11	54	34	1	0
Understanding of myself	19	58	22	1	0
Sense of purpose in life	7	52	39	1	0
Understanding of what life is all about	9	46	42	2	1
Sense that there is inner meaning to my life	7	44	46	1	2
Involvement and positive relations with family	17	44	37	1	1
Concern about what others think of me	3	18	58	20	1
Desire to make a good impression on others	5	25	60	10	0
Death-Related Attitudes					
Fear of death	2	5	67	22	4
Belief in life after death	5	25	67	2	1
Spirituality and Religion					
Interest in organized religion	1	12	80	5	2
Belief in a higher power	4	18	75	2	1
Religious feelings	2	18	77	2	1
Inner sense of God's presence	4	23	71	1	1
Materialism and Other Values					
Concern with material things	2	9	65	21	2
Desire for wealth	5	6	74	13	1
Competitiveness	2	12	74	12	0
Tolerance of violence	1	7	64	22	6

168

TABLE 4: ATTITUDE AND VALUE CHANGES
       AMONG LOVE PROJECT STUDENTS
       ONE YEAR LATER (N=29)

I.	*Overall Effect of Love Project after One Year*	
	Strong, continuing, positive effects	17%
	Some continuing, positive effects	66%
	Very little continuing, positive effects	3%
	No continuing, positive effects	14%

II.	Attitude and Value Changes	% *Increase* Strong	Some	% No Change	% *Decrease* Some	Strong
	Concern for Others					
	Desire to help others	7	57	34	0	0
	Compassion for others	21	52	28	0	0
	Ability to listen patiently to others	14	45	41	0	0
	Tolerance for others	28	41	31	0	0
	Ability to express love openly to others	14	52	34	0	0
	Insight into others' problems	17	55	28	0	0
	Acceptance of others	17	57	24	0	0
	Personal Growth					
	Feelings of self-worth and self-esteem	14	38	48	2	0
	Understanding of myself	10	57	31	0	0
	Sense of purpose in life	7	31	62	0	0
	Understanding of what life is all about	7	52	41	0	0
	Involvement and positive family relations	17	41	41	0	0
	Death-Related Attitudes					
	Fear of death	0	7	66	28	0
	Spirituality and Religion					
	Interest in organized religion	7	21	57	14	0
	Belief in a higher power	7	10	83	0	0
	Religious feelings	7	21	69	2	1
	Inner sense of God's presence	7	21	69	3	0
	Materialism					
	Concern with material things	0	0	76	21	3

Appendixes

1. LOVE PROJECT
GUIDELINES

Though most students had positive experiences with the Love Project, many offered useful suggestions for improving the implementation of the project. These should be taken into account by other academics who want to institute a project either in an existing class or as a separate course.

My own course is still very much in the process of emergence and development. It first took place in a large (150–250 students) class in Introductory Sociology in a lecture hall where it was difficult to carry on discussions and for students to get to know one another and was composed largely of students taking the course as part of a social science university requirement. Many of these problems would be resolved or alleviated if classes were smaller and all students took the course on a voluntary basis. Nonetheless, a number of my students' observations have been very helpful and are relevant to any size or type of class that might use the Love Project idea.

Because it was difficult to have small discussion groups dealing with the project in the large lecture hall and because I had to cover the usual Introductory Sociology material in lectures, many students were initially somewhat confused as to the nature of the project and uneasy about taking part in such an innovative exercise. In addition, in order to allow the spirit of love to work in my students' lives as freely as possibly, I deliberately left the project instructions relatively open-ended, instructing them to relate in a loving manner to someone they wouldn't otherwise relate to, using the *Love* book as a guide.

Though I gave much advice to individual students, and though most of them eventually had no problem finding a suitable person, there was in the first class a considerable amount of uncertainty about expectations, which was alleviated by a clearer set of instructions the second time around. These instructions, which are in this section, clearly spell out the purposes of the project in relation to course material and provide likely sources of persons.

In this regard, it is important for the instructor to have made initial contact with nursing homes, agencies, Big Brother and Big Sister programs, and schools in order to ascertain the extent to which such ongoing programs could be sources of people for the project. For example, more than two dozen students lost a considerable amount of time during one semester owing to a delay in the decision of the local school board officials as to whether or not they could tutor underprivileged students in local schools; the eventual denial of this request discouraged some of the students, who then had relatively little time to find alternative Love Project persons. Thus, since some Love Projects will take place in already structured contexts and as part of ongoing voluntary programs, it is important for the instructor to make the initial groundwork contacts with relevant program directors to make sure that students seeking Love Projects through existing programs will find receptive groups ready to provide them with suitable people.

In addition to such structural groundwork, it is perhaps even more necessary to make sure that students have been adequately prepared in terms of the *spirit* of the project, which is in many respects a substantial departure from the kinds of college classroom assignments students are accustomed to and also, in many respects, contrary to social values and norms. As one student put it:

> I think society is not geared to open affection and "love" communication. I think it is difficult and improbable to expect people, especially students, to instantly react to such an innovative approach. It can cause awkward feelings. Perhaps conferring directly with the students during the term would provide insight on what type of "love communication" they would feel confident and easy about participating in.

Such awkwardness and uncertainty can be alleviated by structuring discussions that gradually lead students to feel more comfortable expressing feelings and relating to others. This, moreover, has the added benefit of helping students, particularly at the freshman level, grow in their capacity to relate to others and overcome shyness.

Another important preparational method is to make sure that students see at least one and preferably two videotapes of Buscaglia lectures and have an opportunity to read and discuss the *Love* book before beginning the project. Those of us with lesser oratorical skills might try to emulate him, but Buscaglia is the acknowledged master at inspiring people to break down the barriers to loving others, and it is essential that students see tapes of his talks. I have found a uniformly strong, positive response to him and a greater understanding of the purposes of the project, especially its underlying spirit, among students after they have listened to him.

Another question that students often raise is whether to inform their project person about the project. I tell the students that, in my experience with hundreds of projects, this has very seldom posed a problem. Students in organized programs need have no qualms about informing people that they are involved in a class project. In less formal contexts, however, it may seem to pose a problem. However, the only problem any student who has completed the project has mentioned is when one project person, an ostracized student, happened to come across my student's notebook. Although the project person was initially somewhat offended to be the object of a course requirement, the personal relationship and genuine interpersonal regard that had built up through the project overrode any ill feelings, because my student could and did sincerely state to her friend that a genuine love did exist between them. In other words, the closeness that develops as a result of a small amount of time relating to the project person quickly creates a genuine relationship, so that it simply doesn't make any difference how my students and their project people got together. The project and course requirement, in other words, is a facilitational device and not an end in itself. As with the objects of NDErs' facilitations, the genuine love that emerges becomes the only thing that is relevant. Thus, though it may sound trite, I simply tell my students to "play it by ear" in terms of telling their project people about the project. And it works, in that no one has ever reported any problems in this regard even after many hundreds of project reports.

Another important issue has to do with the Love Journals that I require the students to keep. Since the project was part of the requirements of standard Introductory Sociology and Social Problems courses, I asked that students interpret their Love Project experiences according to relevant sociological principles. For example, many who related to people from different backgrounds or different ages discussed how culture shock, ethnocentrism, and other barriers that initially led them to feel uneasy with their project persons were overcome through the "I-Thou" relationships that emerged, in ways that enabled the students and project people to relate at the deepest levels of personhood rather than in terms of preexisting stereotypes. Whereas many students discussed how they thereby overcame labeling and other judgmental tendencies, many journals were somewhat shallow in that they often merely recorded interactions in diarylike fashion with a paucity of analysis. In the future, I plan to have a more structured set of requirements for the journals so that students will be motivated to more deeply and thoroughly analyze the larger-scale implications of their project relationships. The same can and should be done for other kinds of courses in which the project might be used, as in psychology.

One of the problems with the fact that the project as I developed it was and is part of existing courses is that students are not motivated fully unless their work has a grade incentive. I have decided to grade the projects on the basis of how deeply and sincerely and thoroughly the student has implemented the project and how well he or she interrelates relevant sociological concepts and perspectives. This is a somewhat unfortunate but necessary aspect of the project, because many students, burdened by the need for attention to be given to grade-related tasks, might otherwise have a tendency to "blow off" or even make up false love Project accounts if the requirement were open-ended. Ideally, the project should be part of a nongraded credit/no-credit class, such as the type Buscaglia teaches at the University of Southern California, but if this is not possible, as it was not for me, grading the students' Love Project journals does provide incentive for students to take the project seriously.

Finally, it is necessary to structure the project requirements somewhat differently for different classes. For my Social Problems classes, for example, I ask that students relate in a loving manner to someone who is representative of a particular social problem—for example, a welfare mother or a lonely elderly person. For my American Minorities course, I tell them to relate to a minority person. In addition, I also include essay questions on exams for these more advanced courses that ask the students to relate how what they have learned through the *Love* book, the relevant lectures and discussions, and their own projects might be used to develop new approaches to social problems.

My experience with the Love Projects suggests that this goal is not necessarily a mere pipe dream. Many of my students, particularly those in more advanced classes, gained insights and understandings of how to deal with individuals who represent various social problems.

2. STUDENT INSTRUCTIONS FOR THE LOVE PROJECT

Purposes

The purposes of the Love Project are (1) to give you a new kind of opportunity for both personal and intellectual growth, (2) to provide you with direct experience of the ways in which social forces relate to and influence the lives of particular individuals, (3) to teach you to relate to others you might not otherwise get to know, (4) to help you gain new insights and think of new ways to deal with social issues and problems, and (5) to let you participate in a new and exciting effort to become more loving and caring and help create a more loving world.

There are many people, some right nearby, desperately in need of love. Such individuals are often victims of social forces that have caused others to label them as unlovable, such as lonely older people, neglected children, members of minority groups, a poor family, a fellow student who doesn't seem to have friends, a custodian in your dorm whom you have noticed but not talked with, or a person from a foreign country who lives nearby. If you need assistance in finding such a person, there are local organizations you can contact, listed below, who can supply you with people who need such help.

In addition to providing a personal growth experience for you and helping you understand sociological concepts and principles, the Love Project can also serve as a basis for exploring career possibilities. Many students have a general interest in a possible career but are not sure whether they would like to pursue, for example, gerontology, juvenile probation work, or social work with the underprivileged. Relating to an older person, a teenager, a younger child in trouble, or an unemployed poor person or family could prove invaluable in helping you decide whether you would be interested in careers dealing with such categories of people. But no matter what your future career, experiencing how to relate to people you wouldn't otherwise relate to will prove very valuable.

Procedures

1. Read *Love* as soon as possible in the semester. This will clarify the overall purposes of the project as well as suggest specific ways to relate to others with love. Keep the book handy, for we will refer to it throughout the semester and use it as a source of insight and inspiration.

2. Find an appropriate person for the project. This may be a "familiar stranger" you may have seen or been aware of, someone you relate to as part of a volunteer program, or someone you already relate to informally but not intensively.

In addition to such informal sources, the Miami University Center for Community Involvement has a wide range of organized programs to help a wide variety of people and could put you in touch with an appropriate person. The Comserv (Community Service) Program of the United Campus Ministry has a need for volunteers to relate to various kinds of people. Your home town minister, priest, or rabbi would be a good source of potential Love Project people. Mrs. Brown, the local welfare coordinator, is also an excellent source of people. In addition, your fraternity, sorority, honorary organization, or other student organization may have a volunteer program of some sort that would be a source for a Love Project person. You may wish to use someone to whom you are already relating in such a program, which is fine—you need not necessarily come up with an entirely "new" person for the project. If you have any questions about how to find an appropriate person, please see Dr. Flynn or Mrs. Marilyn Adams.

3. Once you have found a suitable person, buy a medium-sized notebook and keep an informal Love Journal of how your relationship grows. Though there is no set number of entries or times when you should write in the journal, generally speaking you should probably write in it at least once a week, more frequently if your relationship develops so that you are relating to the person more frequently.

One of the most frequently asked questions is, "Should I tell the person he or she is part of a project?" At first, this may seem to be a problem. After all, human relationships are ideally supposed to emerge spontaneously. There are many times, however, when we think we'd like to get to know some category of person, or particular people, and we just don't have the time or the motivation. Look on the Love Project as your chance to get to know someone you probably wouldn't otherwise have related to but *would have liked to.* Once you think of it this way, the relationship that emerges *is* genuine. After all, you chose the one person out of countless possibilities—there must have been a reason to do so.

Once you realize all this, initial awkwardness quickly dissolves, and the fact that the project gave you an *incentive* to get to know the person becomes irrelevant. The problem with telling project people is not present in volunteer and similar programs, where the person assumes some sort of class-or university-related tie-in. With informal relationships, I have found that as the project develops into a genuine relationship, how it began becomes unimportant. In general, "play it by ear." If you think, in the early stages, that your person's feelings might be hurt, don't tell him or her about the project. But when and if you do, tell the person you are trying to apply Leo Buscaglia's ideas about love in your life and that he or she is one of the people you're "practicing" with. If possible, give them a copy of the book. No one objects to being loved. In many hundreds of instances, no one has told me that their project person has reacted negatively about the project. Several students told me people they were relating to were *temporarily* surprised and somewhat "miffed," but once they thought about it, they realized that the relationship was real and genuine, and the friendships as a result grew even deeper and more meaningful because the project person realized he or she had been consciously singled out for love, which is the greatest compliment anyone can get and the greatest fulfillment one can gain.

In the journal, you should (1) Describe your efforts to relate the ideas in the *Love* book in your emerging relationship with the person. *Love* contains many practical suggestions of how to relate to others in loving ways; (2) Describe the major perceptions and feelings you have about the person and how those feelings, including stereotypes, perceptions, and labels that Buscaglia discusses are a product of your socialization. Discuss how these feelings and perceptions change as you come to know the person not as a social category but as a unique human being; and (3) Use relevant concepts and knowledge from lectures, text, and so on to help you understand both your Love Project person and yourself better but also to deepen and broaden your understanding of the course material. Try to apply concepts, insights, and findings from text chapters and lectures that seem relevant to your Love Project person and your relationship with him or her.

For example, you may find yourself experiencing *culture shock* if you relate to a person from another country or a person from a different social class than your own, and you may initially judge the person negatively because of his or her cultural traits. This should help you get a better understanding of the meaning of cultural differences, which you should discuss in your Love Journal. A journal entry dealing with this might read:

> Yesterday I went to see Mrs. Smith, an elderly black lady, for the first time. She lives in a small house not far from campus. When I went in, I found that she has different kinds of furniture and lives and talks very differently from anyone I've known before. At first, I felt a degree of "culture shock" and experienced an ethnocentric negative reaction, but then I thought of how Buscaglia mentions that we need to avoid labeling people, and as I got to know her better, I began to see Mrs. Smith as a human being despite our outward differences.

This sample entry uses two concepts from the chapter on culture—culture shock and ethnocentrism. Each chapter in your (Introductory Sociology, Social Problems, American Minorities) text contains at least two concepts that can be related to your project interactions. For example, you might see ways in which unemployment and other economic patterns as discussed in one of the chapters are reflected in the life of your Love Project person and then discuss in your journal how the person's life is affected by larger socioeconomic forces, using relevant sociological concepts and theories. Or you may see that the educational, religious, family-related or other experiences or characteristics of your project person are congruent with and reflective of larger-scale institutional patterns as discussed in text, readings, and lecture. As the sociologist C. Wright Mills pointed out, individual's lives reflect "macrocosmic" social-structural forces. Dr. Flynn will, in lectures and discussions, provide many examples of such links between your own and others' lives and the larger socioeconomic and cultural order. Be sure to discuss in your Love Journal any such patterns and insights that occur to you as you are relating to your project person and to indicate whether you see ways in which you and the person can use love as a means for more effectively dealing with the structural patterns that shape our lives and that need not hamper the full flowering of our humanity if we find ways to let unconditional love overcome them.

4. At the end of the term, write at the end of your journal a summation of what the Love Project has meant to you in terms of your personal and intellectual growth. Your grade will not depend on the "success" of your project, so please honestly state how the project has affected your outlook, attitudes, and so forth and how it has contributed to your education, values, and personal life. Though these will be supplemented by anonymous questionnaires, this will help Dr. Flynn develop a more effective Love Project. In addition, summarize how the project has provided you with better understanding of sociological concepts, theories, and findings, and give examples of these.

You need not retype or redo the journal, as long as it is reasonably neat and legible. Please make a xerox copy of the original. Dr. Flynn would like to retain the original in order to study them more carefully later.

Your project will be due one week before the end of classes, so as to give the instructor time to read them carefully. The project will be graded and will count as one-fourth of your final grade. It will be judged on the evidence of the sincerity with which you have undertaken the project, the depth of analysis and insight of a sociological nature you display, and the instructor's assessment of the genuineness of the growth you have undergone. Do not worry if your project person proves hard to get to know; a "successful" project is determined by your effort to apply the lessons of the *Love* book in a sociologically relevant way, rather than by how well the person responds.

PLEASE REMEMBER:

It is important that you start *early in the semester* with the project, because it is *essential* that you develop a relationship of some depth with your project person, and this usually cannot be done hurriedly. Also, if you have trouble with the project, please see and talk with me; I'll be glad to help you.

Above all, let the spirit of love guide you. It's fun!

Bibliography

ALLMAN, WILLIAM F. 1984. Nice guys finish first. *Science 84,* 4 October, 24–32.

ANSBRO, JOHN J. 1984. *Martin Luther King, Jr.: The making of a mind.* Maryknoll, N.Y.: Orbis Books.

ARNOLD, EBERHARD. 1964. *Eberhard Arnold: A testimony of church-community from his life and writings.* Rifton, New York: Plough Publishing House.

BECKER, CARL. 1981. The centrality of Near-Death Experiences in Chinese Pure Land Buddhism. *Anabiosis* 1, no. 2:154–71.

BECKER, ERNEST. 1975. *Escape from evil.* New York: Free Press.

BECKER, ERNEST. 1973. *The denial of death.* New York: Free Press.

BONHOEFFER, DIETRICH. 1963. *The Cost of discipleship.* New York: Macmillan.

BUBER, MARTIN. 1970. *I and Thou.* New York: Scribners.

BUSCAGLIA, LEO. 1982. *Love.* New York: Fawcett.

COLES, ROBERT. 1977. *The privileged ones.* Boston: Little, Brown.

DEWOLF, L. HAROLD. 1953. *A theology of the living church.* New York: Harper.

DURKHEIM, EMILE. 1915. *The elementary forms of the religious life.* London: George Allen and Unwin.

FLYNN, CHARLES P. 1977. *Insult and society: Patterns of comparative interaction.* Port Washington, N.Y.: Kennikat.

GALLAGHER, PATRICK. 1982. Over easy: A cultural anthropologist's Near-Death Experience. *Anabiosis* 2, no. 2:140–49.

GALLUP, GEORGE, JR. 1982. *Adventures in immortality.* New York: McGraw-Hill.

GREYSON, BRUCE. 1981. Near-Death Experiences and attempted suicide. *Sucide and Life-Threatening Behavior* 2:10–16.

HALL, MANLY P. 1951. *The mystical Christ.* Los Angeles: Philosophical Research Society.

HELENE, NINA. 1984. Christian Near-Death Experiences. Unpublished doctoral dissertation, Boston University School of Humanities.

HODES, AUBREY. 1971. *Martin Buber: An intimate portrait.* New York: Viking Press.

JAMES, WILLIAM. 1911. The moral equivalent of war. In *Memories and studies,* 267–96. New York: Longmans, Green.

KNITTER, PAUL. 1985. *No other name?* Maryknoll, N.Y.: Orbis Books.

LAHAYE, TIM. 1980. *Life in the afterlife.* Wheaton, Illinois: Tyndale House.

LEWIS, C.S. 1955. *Surprised by joy.* New York: Harcourt, Brace.

LODER, JAMES. 1981. *The transforming moment: Understanding convictional experiences.* New York: Harper and Row.

MILLER, ALICE. 1983. *For your own good.* New York: Farrar, Straus, Giroux.

MOODY, RAYMOND A.,J. 1975. *Life after life.* Covington, Georgia: Mockingbird Books, 1977. *Reflections on life after life.* Covington, Georgia: Mockingbird Books.

NIEBUHR, REINHOLD. 1953. *The nature and destiny of man.* New York: Charles Scribner's Sons.

NOYES, RUSSELL. 1982. The human experience of death. *Omega* 13:251–59.

NYGREN, ANDERS. 1932; 1969. *Agape and eros.* New York: Harper and Row.

OLIVE, DON. 1973. *Wolfhart Pannenberg.* Waco, Tex.: Word Books.

OSIS, KARLIS, and HARALDSSON, ERLENDUR. 1977. *At the hour of death.* New York: Avon.

PASAROW, REINEE. 1981. A personal account of an NDE. *Vital Signs* 1, no. 3: 11–14.

PATTERSON, BOB E. 1977. *Reinhold Niebuhr.* Waco, Tex.: Word Books.

PETERS, THOMAS J., and WATERMAN, ROBERT H., JR. 1982. *In search of excellence.* New York: Harper and Row.

RAWLINGS, MAURICE. 1978. *Beyond death's door.* Nashville, Tennessee: Thomas Nelson.

RING, KENNETH. 1980. *Life at death.* New York: Coward, McCann and Geoghegan.

———. 1984. *Heading toward Omega.* New York: Morrow.

RITCHIE, GEORGE, with ELIZABETH SHERRILL. 1978. *Return from tomorrow.* Waco, Tex.: Word Books.

SABOM, MICHAEL. 1982. *Recollections of death.* New York: Harper and Row.

SABOM, MICHAEL, and KREUTZIGER, SARAH. 1977. The Experience of Near Death. *Death Education.* I: 193–203.

SCHELL, JONATHAN. 1982. *The fate of the earth.* New York: Knopf.

SOROKIN, PITIRIM. 1967. *The ways and power of love.* Chicago: Henry Regnery.

SPINK, KATHRYN. 1984. *I need souls like you.* New York: Harper and Row.

SWIHART, PHILLIP J. 1978. *The edge of death.* Downers Grove, Illinois: Intervarsity Press.

TAYLOR, DARLENE. 1981. Profile of an experiencer: Joe Geraci. *Vital Signs* 1, no. 3:3–12.

WHITE, JOHN. 1981. Jesus, evolution, and the future of humanity. *Science of Mind*, September (a) and October (b), 8–17, 40–108.

WOLFE, THOMAS. 1938. *You can't go home again.* New York: Harper.

Index

A

Adams, Marilyn, 123
Adventures in Immortality (Gallup), 2, 16
Adopt-a-Grandparent, 122
Afterlife:
  assumption of, 152
  increased belief in, 34, 55, 58
  after Love Project, 124
Agape:
  on an individual level, 148, 154–55
  meaning and fulfillment through, 147
  and NDE, 72
  versus Eros, 141
Agape and Eros (Nygren), 72
Agnosticism, and transformation to belief in God, 66, 73
non-NDEr's transformation to agnosticism, 63

"A.J.," 44–49
Allman, William F., 154
Anabiosis (IANDS), 2
Arnold, Eberhard, 158
Atchley, Robert, 133

B

Becker, Ernest, 3, 5, 77, 147, 154
Bonhoeffer, Dietrich, 73–74
Booth, William, 72
Brahma, union with, 76
Buber, Martin, 71, 72
Buddha, and difference between Christ, 94–95
Buddhism, congruencies of with NDE, 76–77
Buscaglia, Leo, 7, 120–21, 141, 156, 157–58, 173, 175

Bush, Nancy Evans, 30

C

Caputo, Philip, 146
Career:
  changes to volunteerism, 102, 103,
    105
  devaluation of importance of, 34, 36
Child abuse, 141
Christian perspective, NDE from,
    80–99
Christmas Carol, A (Dickens), 50
Church involvement after an NDE,
    81–82
  See also Religious meaning of NDE
    for experiencer
Clairvoyance after NDE, 31
Clark, Kimberly, 20, 83–86, 87
Clark, Nancy, 6, 67–68, 82, 87, 91,
    110–17
Clinical death, 2, 95
Communication, problems of after
    NDE, 16–18, 20
Compassion, as after-effect of NDE,
    5, 7, 34, 37, 44, 60, 61, 64
  in Buddhism, 76–77
  passed on to children of NDErs, 109
  promulgation of through Love
    Project, 157
Competitive success, indifference to,
    34, 37–39
Contemplation of death, effect of on
    values, 51
1 Corinthians, 158
2 Corinthians, 80, 86, 93, 99
Cost of Discipleship, The (Bonhoeffer),
    73

D

Death, fear of:
  decreased after Love Project, 124,
    144
  decreased after NDE, 5, 34, 54, 61,
    103, 117
  increased, 56, 58, 60
Death of Ivan Illych, The (Tolstoy),
    50
Denial of Death (Becker), 3
Divorce, as after-effect of NDE, 24

E

Elderly, ability to relate to after Love
    Project, 131–34
Ephesians 4, 156
Escape from Evil (Becker), 3

F

For Your Own Good (Miller), 141

G

Gallagher, Patrick, 12, 13, 66
Gallup, George, Jr., 2, 16
Gandhi, Mahatma, 141
Geraci, Joe, 35–36, 154
Gerontology, interest in as a result of
    Love Project, 125, 133
Golden Rule moral consciousness,
    heightened, 38
Grace:
  divine, 91, 96, 97
  true versus "cheap," 73–74
  universal, 91–99
Greyson, Bruce, 20, 56, 57–58, 64

H

Hall, Manly P., 162
Hallucinations, NDEs thought of as,
    16–17
Haraldsson, Erlendur, 74–75
Harris, Barbara, 34, 77, 103, 105–6,
    117
  spiritual transformation of, 69–71

Heading toward Omega (Ring), 31, 61, 76

Hegelian Idealism, 74

Helene, Nina, 80

Hell, NDErs perception of, 82, 86

Hinduism, and NDEs, 75, 76

Hitler, Adolf, 141

Home on earth, finding within people, 152

Hunting, aversion to among male NDErs, 40

I

IANDS, *see* International Association for Near-Death Studies

Immortality striving, 3–4, 5, 74, 154
  and Resurrection of Christ, 153

Immortality vehicles, 3
  children as, 4

Indian NDEs, 74–75, 76

International Association for Near-Death Studies, 2, 5, 20, 30, 44, 57

I-Thou relationships, 72, 157
  during wartime, 147

J

James, William, 147

Japanese kamikaze pilots, 147

Jesus Christ:
  and the Light, 3, 92–93, 94, 96, 98
  as a specimen of new form of humanity, 155

Judeo-Christian theology, implications of NDE for, 71–74
  agape, 72
  divine revelation, 74
  grace, true versus "cheap," 73–74

Judgmentalism, diminished, 29–30

Juvenile delinquents, NDErs attempts to help, 108

K

King, Dr. Martin Luther, Jr., 141, 153, 157
  vision of future of humanity, 148–49

Kingdom of God on earth, 152, 158

Knitter, Paul, 93

Knowledge, as after-effect of NDE, 10, 12, 26–27

Kohlberg, Lawrence, 158

Koran, messages of, similarities to NDE, 77

Kreutziger, Sarah, 56, 58

Kübler-Ross, Elisabeth, 17, 51

Kundalini experience, relevance to NDE, 76

L

La Haye, Tim, 86

Les Miserables (Hugo), 50

Lewis, C. S., 72

Light:
  Being of, 2, 10, 76, 121
  crystal cities, 10
  experiences of, 10–11, 47–48, 74, 83, 85, 88
  forgiveness of, 3
  God as, 90, 93, 110–11, 115
  judgment of, 83
  knowledge and, 10, 12
  living in, 152–59
  love and, 11, 114–15, 116, 149, 154, 158, 162
  message of, 7
  relatives, communication with, 41
  return from, choice of, 13
  as universal Christ, 81–99
  value changes and, 35
  See also Jesus Christ, and the Light

Life at Death (Ring), 2

Life after Life (Moody), 2, 18, 47, 80

Life review, as part of NDE, 10, 11–12
Life-threatening situations, effects of,
    54–62
  achievement orientation, 55
  negative reactions to, 55
  risks, attitudes towards, 55
  suicide, 56–57
  survivors, attitudes of, 57–64
Loder, James, 73, 86
Love (Buscaglia), 7, 120, 124, 142,
    144, 172, 173
Love Project, 8, 120–49, 152, 154–59,
    163
  ability to break down social,
    economic, and age barriers,
    125–26, 131, 144–45
  attitude and value changes among
    participants, tables, 168–69
  Buscaglia's tapes, 123
  capacity for compassion and love,
    growth in, 125–27
  Christian faith, enhancement of, 142,
    155–57
  disclosure of to project person,
    120–21, 173–74, 177
  elderly, ability to relate to, 131–34
  genuineness of relationships, 122
  growth in concern for others, as
    result, 123, 124
  guidelines for, 172–75
  instructions for students, 175–80
  journals, 174–75
  love as a means of bringing about
    change, 141, 148–49, 155–57
  as means of career exploration,
    122–23, 125, 176
  questionnaires, follow-up, 144
  origins, 120–21
  perceptions, changes in, 128–29
  personal growth, as a result of, 123
  prejudice, ability to overcome, 134
  religious attitudes, changes in,
    123–24
  self-worth, increase in, 124
  social skills, enhancement of, 129–30
  sources for project people, 122,
    172–73
  "superiority" and "inferiority,"
    transcending, 145–46
  Universal Christ, 157
Love, unconditional, 7, 24, 110–11,
    114–15, 116–18, 120, 154
  cosmic order of, 158
  brotherhood of humanity, 148–49
  as element of world religions, 141–42
  God as, 99, 111
  law of, 148
  as natural religion of mankind, 162
  transforming power of, 142
  See also Agape

M

Material success, indifference to, 34,
    35–37
  after Love Project, 144
Meaning of life, through acts of
    kindness, 34–35, 152–53
Miller, Alice, 141
Miller, Sheila, 133
Mills, C. Wright, 179
Moody, Raymond, 2, 3, 18, 57, 80, 86
Mother Teresa, 69, 82, 97, 157

N

NDEs/NDErs:
  agape and, 72
  attitude and value changes, table, 166
  common experiences of, 2, 10
  communicating, problems of, 16–18
  death, fear of, 5

as a demonic deception, 5, 80, 84, 88, 90

effects of on others, 6–7, 44–51

enlightenment after, 26

family reactions to, 16, 17, 24

guidelines for helping NDErs, 20–21

helping others, desire for, 6, 34–35, 36, 41–42, 46–50, 58, 102–18, 153

human evolution, as new stage of, 7, 163

judgmentalism, diminished, 29–30

life review, 11–12

love and, 2, 6, 24, 50, 104, 110–11, 112–15, 116

meaning of life, enhanced sense of, 67

morality of, 3, 38

NDErs versus non-NDErs, 54–64

negative experiences, 82–86, 87

non-Western, 74–78

personal growth after, 26, 27–28

psychic powers after, 31–32, 149

reality of, 14

relatives, encounters with, 10, 12–13

resocializaton after, 27

return from, 13

reverence for life after, 39–40

self-righteousness, diminished, 29

sharing, difficulties of, 16–21

skepticism about, 4–5

suicide and, 56–57

war, ways in which NDE can help overcome, 146–47

See also Afterlife; Compassion, as after-effect of NDE; Death, fear of; Religious meaning of NDE for experiencer; Universal Christ, NDErs belief in; Values, changes in

Niebuhr, Reinhold, 148, 149, 152

Non-NDE survivors, attitude and value changes, 167

Nonviolence, Hindu emphasis on and NDE, 76

Noyes, Russell, 54–55

Nygren, Anders, 72

O

Osis, Karlis, 74–75

Our Town (Wilder), 50

P

Pannenberg, Wolfhart, 74

Pasarow, Reinee, 12

Peretz, Isaac Loeb, 71

Peters, Thomas J., 154

Places in the Heart, 158

Prayer, increase in after NDE, 67

Precognition after NDE, 31

Psychic powers of NDErs, 31–32, 149

R

Rawlings, Maurice, 86

Recollections of Death (Sabom), 56

Relationships, changes in after NDE, 24–25, 117

Religion, organized, teachings of, 3

NDErs attitude towards, 68–69

Religious meaning of NDE for experiencer, 43–44, 46, 49

closeness to God, 67–68

conversion to Christianity, 87–91

direct knowledge of God, 66

divine love and, 69, 99

grace, universal, 91

Judeo-Christian theology, 71–74

non-NDErs, experiences of, 62, 63

non-Western, 74–78

organized religion, 68

Religious meaning of NDE for
   experiencer (*cont.*)

spiritual transformations, 66–71,
   110–11

See also Jesus Christ, and the Light;
   Universal Christ, NDErs belief in

Researchers, role of, 19

Resocialization, after NDE, 27

Reverence for life, 39–40

Ring, Kenneth, 2, 5–6, 10, 19, 31, 35,
   56, 76, 103

Ritchie, George, 80

Ritter, Father, 82

Roberts, Nancy, 146

S

Sabom, Michael, 2, 56, 58

Saint Augustine, 149, 162

Sawyer, Elaine, 25

Sawyer, Timmy, 109–10

Sawyer, Tom, 6, 24, 26, 29, 32, 34, 37,
   38, 49, 66, 73, 81, 91

Schell, Jonathan, 146

Schweitzer, Dr. Albert, 39

Scripps Foundation, 133

Self-actualized people, 154

Self-righteousness, diminished, 29

Seltzer, Mildred, 133

Sorokin, Pitirim, 120

Spiritual transformations of NDErs, *see*
   Religious meaning of NDE for
   experiencer

Staccato, Mickey, 12, 41–44

Suicide attempters, transformations
   among NDErs and non-NDErs,
   56–57, 114

Surprised by Joy (Lewis), 73

Swihart, Phillip, 86

T

Terminally ill, NDErs ability to help
   and empathy with, 102–4

Tibetan Book of the Dead, 77

Transforming Moment, The (Loder),
   73

Tunnel, experience of moving through,
   2, 10–11, 82

U

Universal Christ, NDErs belief in, 7,
   80–81, 157

church involvement, 81–82

V

Values, changes in, 24–25, 34–37, 42

Violence, increased sensitivity to,
   39–40

Vital Signs (IANDS), 2

W

War, ways in which NDE can help
   overcome, 146–47

mythology of war, 147

Waterman, Robert H., Jr., 154

Ways and Power of Love (Sorokin),
   120

Wealth, pursuit of, 4

Wesley, John, 72

White, John, 154–55

Winner, Elaine, 6, 10–11, 13, 30, 34,
   35, 82, 90, 102

Wolfe, Thomas, 152